CLAUDETTE SARTILIOT

HERBARIUM
═══
VERBARIUM

The Discourse of Flowers

The University of Nebraska Press

Lincoln & London

Library of Congress Cataloging
in Publication Data
Sartiliot, Claudette, 1945–
Herbarium / verbarium: the discourse of flowers /
Claudette Sartiliot.   p. cm.—
(Texts and contexts: v. 7)
Includes bibliographical references and index.
ISBN 0-8032-4229-8 (cloth: alka-
line paper)
1. Flowers in literature. 2. Symbolism of flowers.
3. Literature, Modern – 20th
century – History
and criticism. I. Title II.Series.
PN56.F55S27 1993
809'.9336 – dc20 93-9530 CIP

for Philip

Contents

Acknowledgments

I would like to thank
Leah Hewitt **&** Sander Gilman for
their constructive comments
on the manuscript. I particularly want to
thank Jacques Derrida, Hélène
Cixous, Renée Riese Hubert, Alexander Gelley,
Gabrielle Schwab **&** Frederick
Dolan for their friendship **&** concern, **&** Stephanie
Davolos **&** Claire Fish for their
valuable help with technical matters. I address my
special thanks to Philip Kuberski
who read **&** commented on the manuscript in
its various stages. A previous
version of the first chapter was published
as 'Herbarium, Verbarium: The
Discourse of Flowers' in *Diacritics* 18,
no.4 (Winter 1988):
68–81. It is included here with
the permission
of the Johns Hopkins
University
Press

Introduction

I had already drawn from the visible stratagems of flowers a conclusion that bore upon a whole unconscious element of literary production. – Marcel Proust

This book is both a theoretical and a practical investigation into the relationship between natural and literary languages, between the reproduction and representation of plant life and the reproduction and representation of mental life. The focus of this investigation is the flower, both as a botanical and as a literary phenomenon. This traditional link between literature and botany – reflected in the works of Goethe, Rousseau, Ruskin, Rilke, Proust, Jean Genet, Francis Ponge, Hélène Cixous, and in the theories of Jacques Derrida, Gilles Deleuze, and Felix Guattari and others – provides a context for examining so-called patriarchal or logocentric representations of the feminine and flowers and for redefining the accepted notion of literary organicism.

The underlying assumption of the book is that critics have generally misunderstood the ways in which literature and literary language are 'organic,' understanding this word as little more than a synonym for the notion of aesthetic unity or totalization that Aristotle introduced, the romantics developed, and New Critics formalized. The aim of this book is to establish a more specific understanding of the organic metaphor by exploring the means by which flowers reproduce and how natural reproduction, allied with contemporary theoretical conceptions of the text, helps us to grasp the ways in which texts, especially modernist and postmodernist ones, are indeed 'organic' in a way quite alien to the idealized view of theory – that is, they belong to a world of dissemination, difference, and metamorphoses.

My approach to these themes has been partly influenced by Derrida's interpretation of the floral and botanical nature of texts. In his essay 'White Mythology,' for example, Derrida uses the example of the flower to demonstrate the similarity of natural and metaphorical languages, of botanical and literary propagation. In *Dissémination,* he calls upon the vocabulary and concepts of botany to demonstrate that in texts, as in the natural world, meaning is not produced in a linear and teleological manner, but rather as a result of an alliance between rule and chance, of a scattering and gathering of 'semes' (seeds and signs). In *Glas,* Derrida shows how flowers reveal an originless chain of metamorphoses, subverting the neat relationship between signifier and signified, and point to a process of signification that cannot be limited to a single, dominant model.

A reading of those texts linking literature and botany – rarely commented upon – led me to investigate the appearance of flowers in texts, and to realize that something other than mere ornamentation or symbolization was involved. Instead of asking the traditional question (what do flowers symbolize?), I consider where they come from and what motivates their appearances. This work then articulates a scattering of writers in whose work there is a marked predilection for flowers, plants, and fruit, works in which the vegetable performs a role far exceeding the decorative or symbolic functions usually recognized, suggesting, instead, a truly organic, creative abundance of significances.

Thus I concentrate mainly on modernist and postmodernist writers who detach the flower from a rigid symbolic and ornamental tradition to reveal its polyvalent and extravagant nature, its verbal, psychological, and botanical significances. In stressing the relationship between literary production and natural production, between psychological and floral revelations, these writers uncover the working of the unconscious and the signifier rather than repressing it, and they present the literary work as fundamentally disseminative and differential. To demonstrate this characteristic of twentieth-century literature, this study relies on the precedence of the classical floral tradition of the emblematic uses of flowers, which culminated in the nineteenth-century social & literary genre of 'the language of flowers.'

In antiquity, when the various realms of knowledge were still linked to one another, and human beings were more aware of their physical and spiritual participation in the natural world, the symbolization of flowers was less systematic. By the Renaissance, however, flowers had become, on the one hand the object of scientific study and on the other, mere literary emblems with fixed meanings. Thus, whenever a lily appeared in a painting or in a poem, its meaning was clear: it signified 'purity,' 'virginity,' or 'innocence' – all of which are conceptual synonyms. In Giovanni Bellini's painting *The Annunciation,* for instance, color and association are fixed and purely conceptual: Gabriel offers the Virgin less a lily than a sign. Similarly, in Shakespeare's plays & poetry, flowers are used for their poetic resonances and their fixed emblematic values: they are aesthetic objects divorced from their natural setting. In *Hamlet,* mad Ophelia distributes a variety of flowers to express her grief about her father's death as well as the feelings of other dramatis personae. Her cryptic message, revealing her motivation in attributing a particular flower to a particular character, can be decoded by the characters, the readers, and the critics according to their knowledge of traditional floral language. When they appear in such lists, such verbalized flowers resemble the ornamental *verdure* of medieval & Renaissance tapestries – they belong exclusively to the world of representation. In Ronsard's poetry, the rose is even more indiscriminate. Even if the poet invites Marie, Cassandre, or Hélène to go and see a rose in a garden, the rose exists nowhere but in the poet's mind as a symbol of love and ephemerality. Ronsard's *rose* is merely a word which, in the French language, fortunately is also a color (pink), and resonates in other words such as *rosée* (dew) and *arrose* (to water).

These imaginary equivalences culminated in the nineteenth-century fashion of 'language of flowers' books. Obscure in origin, these treatises were devised to allow lovers to put together a bouquet of flowers to express their secret love. Obviously, the message was far more important than the flowers. In fact, one could send a poem instead of a bouquet: the names of the flowers were sufficient and, of course, more lasting than their perfumed but ephemeral equivalents.[1] After all, as Baudelaire well knew, a flower was another name for a poem: anthologies were cut flowers and reading a gathering (of flowers). How tempting therefore to name a volume of poetry *Les Fleurs du mal,* to associate flowers with pain and evil, to break with the tradition in which human beings used natural elements as verbal signs, to return to the mythological and ambivalent notion that nature – not culture – has always expressed itself in its own way.

If flowers are generally associated with women, beauty, innocence, and passivity, one realizes that, far from letting themselves be reduced to these adequations, flowers appear as having no stable *topos*. In texts, as in the natural world, they are alive with stratagems, devoted to metamorphoses and mimicries: they can easily be turned into their opposites and thus express the feminine, the masculine, or both – they can even show the artificiality of their opposition, and of opposition in general. Thus the floral dimension of texts often subverts not only linearity but identity as such, and gender in particular. The flower, traditionally viewed as a symbol of passive receptivity, can thus be seen as a radical trope and life-form, whose appearances in modernist and postmodernist texts this book seeks to trace.

The first chapter, 'The Discourse of Flowers,' starts with a reading of Georges Bataille's 'The Language of Flowers.' After trying to explain why flowers emblematize certain human qualities, Bataille discovers the relationship between flowers and the unconscious. Next, my reading of Freud's 'dream of the botanical monograph' demonstrates the complex links between the flower and the unconscious, & the disturbances that the flower creates in Freud's analysis – especially the impossibility of making the flower serve as a neat illustration of a psychoanalytic idea. Chapter 1 develops the relationship between the flower and the letter, between the herbarium and the verbarium. It reveals that flowers indicate a nodal point in texts which undermines the hermeneutic enterprise and offers an alternative model of signification that takes into account what has been repressed by logocentric systems of thought, namely plurality, the signifier, the unconscious, the feminine. The chapter examines the relationship between the generation of meaning in nature and literature. Botanist Jean-Marie Pelt's metaphor of the postal service, establishing how natural reproduction happens according to the play of randomness and rule, is juxtaposed with Jacques Derrida's use of a similar metaphor explaining the production of meaning in literature—as well as the destination and reception of the text.

Both in the scientific and literary domains, the flower is associated with vision. If the flower is beautiful this is so it can be seen by humans or by insects – depending on the theory. This means forgetting, on the one hand, that other senses come into play in the vegetable world besides vision, and on the other hand, that the flower has its roots in the underground, the realm of night and death. The second chapter, 'Writing from the Underworld,' focuses on Proust's & Rilke's descent into this underworld of the unconscious out of which the work of art is supposed to arise. It concentrates on Marcel's attitude toward flowers and especially on his account of the meeting of the Baron de Charlus and Jupien which Proust modeled on the encounter between orchids and bees – a story told by Charles Darwin. From this encounter, Marcel learns about the organic nature of the work of art, and about the fertilization of the mind of the artist by the outside world. Vision in Proust is therefore not the mastering vision of scientific specialization; it is rather a complex experience in which subject and object are merged and in which inside and outside interpenetrate. In Rilke, especially in the *Sonnets to Orpheus,* the flower is associated with the ear; flowers and ears represent thresholds between inside and outside, above and underneath. For Rilke, flowers and women are teachers who should liberate men from their attachment to the world of reasoned vision, and show them how to belong to the world, rather than being mere spectators of it. This chapter demonstrates that flowers appeal to writers who want to reconcile subject and object, to find a correspondence between human beings and the world.

Coming back to the surface again, leaving the unconscious behind, the third chapter, 'The Manufacture of the Meadow,' analyzes a single poem, Francis Ponge's 'Le Pré.' Ponge, who usually writes about objects, seems to privilege the 'natural,' because he finds a correlation between generation in the natural world and the generation of a poem. Ponge's poem attempts to take the *pré* (meadow), a psychological, literary *topos,* back to its natural, realistic, and objective origin. If his poem reads like a prosaic ecological treatise, it is because he wants to relinquish the romantic and pastoral representation of the *pré* in order to present it to us as part of our ordinary world – a world in which twentieth-century men and women still have to live. This is why Ponge presents the *pré* as our beginning and our end, and stresses the relationship between our nature and nature, between the differential nature of language and the differential language of nature.

The last chapter, 'The Flower, the Fruit, the Feminine,' concentrates on the work of Hélène Cixous as a means of considering the relationship between the flower & the feminine with which we started. An analysis of works by Cixous, especially *Illa* & *Limonade tout était si infini,* helps to conceptualize and flesh out the relationship between woman and the natural world. Using the myth of Demeter and Persephone, Cixous underlines the ancient proximity between the mother (earth) and the daughter (fruit of the earth). If Cixous accepts the traditional association between flowers and women, it is because she wants to liberate both from the mastering masculine gaze & show the relationship between women & the mother earth, a relationship obscured by scientific specialization and by a kind of feminism still bound by oppositional thinking.

CHAPTER ONE

The Discourse of Flowers

I say a flower! and from that forgetfulness to which my voice consigns all contours, as something other than the known calyxes, musically arises the smiling and lofty idea, that is absent from all bouquets. – Mallarmé

Because of their perfume, shape, color, in short, because of their 'beauty,' flowers have traditionally served as a common literary device to express human qualities. In 'Le Langage des fleurs' (The Language of Flowers), Georges Bataille gives examples of the human characteristics that flowers have been supposed to emblematize. Thus, the dandelion signifies expansion; the narcissus, egotism; absinthe, bitterness; the rose, love; and the water lily, indifference. Bataille, who searches for a rational explanation of the relationship between flowers and what they symbolize, believes that he can find one concerning the examples just given.

Si le pissenlit signifie expansion, le narcisse égoïsme ou l'absinthe amertume, on en voit trop facilement la raison. Il ne s'agit pas visiblement d'une divination du sens secret des fleurs, et l'on discerne immédiatement la propriété bien connue ou la légende qu'il a suffi d'utiliser.

If the dandelion signifies expansion, the narcissus egotism, or absinthe bitterness, one can too easily see why. The meaning

does not obviously derive from a divination of the secret mean-
ing of the flowers, and it is easy to perceive immediately the
well-known property or the legend used.[1]

Since Bataille tries to explain rationally the link between certain flowers and what they have come to symbolize, it is surprising that here he should be satisfied with an explanation that has hardly anything to do with flowers. Indeed, the link between the *pissenlit* (which also means 'wet-the-bed') and expansion is purely linguistic and clear only in French, even though it is derived from the properties of the flower itself. In English, for instance, the common name is 'dandelion,' derived from the French *dent de lion* (lion's tooth), which has nothing to do with 'bedwetting' and expansion but rather results from an interpretation of the shape of the leaves of the plant. Similarly, the relationship between the flower narcissus and 'egotism' is established through the myth of Narcissus, another kind of translation. Yet that flower's name may actually have nothing to do with the mythical Narcissus, as is commonly believed.[2] Bataille is willing to accept these explanations because the relationships they present are motivated and reasonable rather than absolutely arbitrary.

Even though Bataille is uneasy about the relationship between actual flowers and their associations, he makes an important point about this apparently arbitrary relationship. After trying to find a rational explanation of the link between flowers and the expression of love, Bataille comes to realize that the relationship between flowers and their symbolic meaning, rather than being motivated or rational, is akin to the kinds of substitutions one encounters in dreams. Of course, in all these cases – and in most others – the flower as flower is absent, as in 'l'absente de tous bouquets' in Mallarmé, or, as Jacques Derrida puts it in *Glas*, 'la fleur est partie.'[3]

Besides symbolizing elements with which they have little to do, flowers are traditionally associated with beauty, innocence, virginity, indifference, and passivity. For instance, in the section on natural religion in *The Phenomenology of Spirit,* Hegel discusses the movement from the religion of flowers to the religion of animals in these terms:

Die Unschuld der Blumenreligion, *die nur selbstlose Vorstellung des Selbsts ist, geht in die Ernst des kämpfenden Lebens, in die Schuld der* Tierreligion, *die Ruhe und Ohnmacht der anschauenden Individualität in das zerstörende Fürsichsein über.*

The innocence of the flower religion, *which is merely the selfless idea of self, gives place to the earnestness of warring life, to the guilt of* animal religion; *the passivity and impotence of contemplative individuality pass into destructive being-for-self.*[4]

One recognizes here the traditional notion of the flower as innocent & indifferent, innocent because indifferent, because selfless, steeped in absolute externality, & unconscious of its concept. Flowers are, in this dialectic, merely a necessary step which, through the work of the negativity of animal religion, will lead to further closeness to the spiritual. It is therefore not surprising that flowers should be associated with women, as they are in Hegel's *Philosophy of Right,* where the difference between men and women is marked by the difference between plants and animals.

Der Unterschied zwischen Mann und Frau ist der des Tieres und der Pflanze: das Tier entspricht mehr dem Charakter des Mannes, die Pflanze mehr dem der Frau, denn sie ist mehr ruhiges Entfalten, das die unbestimmtere Einigkeit der Empfindung zu seinem Prinzip erhält. Stehen Frauen an der Spitze der Regierung, so ist der Staat in Gefahr, denn sie handeln nicht nach der Anforderung der Allgemeinheit, sondern nach zufälliger Neigung und Meinung. Die Bildung der Frauen geschieht, man weiß nicht wie, gleichsam durch die Atmosphäre der Vorstellungen, mehr durch das Leben als durch das Er-

werben von Kenntnissen, während der Mann seine Stellung nur durch die Errungenschaft des Gedankens und durch viele technische Bemühungen erlangt.

The difference between men and women is like that between animals and plants. Men correspond to animals, while women correspond to plants because their development is more placid and the principle that underlies it is the rather vague unity of feeling. When women hold the helm of government, the state is at once in jeopardy, because women regulate their actions not by the demands of universality but by arbitrary inclinations and opinions. Women are educated – who knows how? – as it were by breathing in ideas, by living rather than by acquiring knowledge. The status of manhood, on the other hand, is attained only by the stress of thought and much technical exertion.[5]

If, within the scope of classical rhetoric, flowers appear as a necessary supplement or ornament, within the Hegelian dialectical confrontation they appear as a dangerous supplement, as that which Hegel would rather exclude from a system whose closure and reasonable purity they threaten. Women as plants are a threat because they fall outside or beyond the scope of knowledge, whose delicate elaboration they endanger mainly through their reliance on the arbitrary and the intuitional. In the foregoing passage, plants and animals are metaphors, displacements, or translations for the opposition between self and non-self, between for-itself & for-others, between passivity & activity, between the male and female principles. The threat is evident in Hegel's surprise at woman's education: 'who knows how?' Women are dangerous because one does not know how they become educated. It seems that they are able, like plants, to educate themselves *by themselves,* by 'breathing in ideas, by living rather than by acquiring knowledge,' in which case they definitely fall outside the boundaries of Absolute Knowledge. To ward off their threat, Hegel then has to turn women either into ornaments or into the example by which he can construct the difference between the sexes. This move is convenient since it allows Hegel to treat woman not as a sex but only as the difference that marks the difference between the sexes.

Even if the role of women and plants seems to be merely to mark the difference between the male and female principles, women (and plants) seem to have a specific role in the scheme of things, albeit a passive one, namely to ensure the destiny of the family, to be imbued with family piety. It is therefore significant that, when Hegel discusses the difference between men and women and between their respective roles, he should mention Antigone. The appearance of Antigone in Hegel's discussion of the difference between the male and female principles, and about the difference between plants and animals, exposes significant links between the feminine, the flower, and knowledge.

Within the Hegelian text, Antigone represents the intrusion of the literary, the feminine, the disseminative into the patriarchal world of order, teleology, & closure, which can neither assimilate her nor, as we shall see, forget or exclude her. Indeed, if it is not surprising that Antigone should appear in Hegel's discussion of tragedy in the *Aesthetics,* her appearance in *The Philosophy of Right* and in *The Phenomenology of Spirit* is more disturbing. There she seems out of place and disrupts the elaboration of the dialectical opposition between the masculine and the feminine, innocence and crime, the passive and the active, revealing the inability of the system either to maintain these oppositions or to relegate the flower, woman, and the unconscious to a secondary role.

What prompts me to read the figure of Antigone as a flower in the Hegelian text is not simply the fact that Hegel introduces her in his discussion of the difference between the sexes indicated by the difference between plants and animals, or the fact that Hegel describes Antigone metaphorically as a flower. What is much more interesting is that the presence of Antigone in the Hegelian text typifies the disturbances created by flowers in texts.

At first, Hegel uses Antigone to exemplify the passive role of woman, especially woman as flower, as defined in the flower religion. As a representative and preserver of the divine law, Antigone has her roots (*Wurzeln*) in the Underworld. As a flower, Antigone belongs to the womb of the earth, to which she must return after accomplishing her fate above it. She is also linked to the earth through the burial rites she performs in accordance with the law of the gods and family piety.

Moreover, like a flower, Antigone is represented as a virgin: she is a virgin and dies a virgin. Even after botanists 'discovered' the sexuality of plants, plants have been – and still are – preferably considered as above or beyond sexuality. How else could the traditional metaphor of their innocence be sustained? Perhaps innocence, in the scientific world as well as in the philosophical world, depends on a denial of sexuality, unless it is a denial of femininity. Hegel's *Philosophy of Right* and Goethe's 'Metamorphose der Pflanzen' are characterized by this repression of sexuality in the plant kingdom. In accordance with the traditional characterization of flowers as sexless and pure, Antigone seems to be involved in a world in which sex, and therefore sin, is absent or repressed: her attachment to her brother, which she deems above her attachment to her future husband Haemon, is not of a sexual nature. This quiet asexual attachment is what Hegel finds *apaisant* (reassuring), as Derrida remarks in *Glas* (GL 169a; 150a).

While discussing Hegel's fascination with Antigone and his privileging of the relationship between brother and sister, Derrida stresses that the appearance of Antigone constitutes a blind spot and rupture in Hegel's logic and system. Indeed, when Hegel quotes from Sophocles' tragedy *Antigone* in *The Phenomenology of Spirit*, he makes her words his own: he lets her speak through his text. Derrida reads this rupture in the Hegelian discourse as the inevitable return of the repressed: 'Où a-t-il donc pris qu'un frère ne peut être remplacé? de la bouche d'Antigone, bien sûr. Elle n'est pas nommée mais elle dicte les énoncés' (GL 168a). ['So where did he get the idea that a brother cannot be replaced? From the mouth of Antigone, of course. She is not named, but she dictates the statements' (GL 165a)].[6] This 'graft' of Antigone's words onto Hegel's discourse indicates for Derrida the inability of the system to close itself upon itself or to silence the unconscious with which the flower, woman, and the signifier are associated.

More important, this graft shows that Antigone, as a woman, as a flower, cannot be confined to the role assigned to her. If, therefore, Antigone appears in Hegel's text as an example of the passive role of woman, this equivalence cannot be maintained, and Antigone eventually brings confusion to the finely delineated oppositions that she was supposed to mark. Antigone is thus, on the one hand, feminine, passive, and innocent as she obeys the rules of family piety and the divine law; however, she is also masculine and a criminal: she opposes the law of the state, to which the individual is supposed to surrender as to a higher ethical dimension. In this case, Hegel is prepared, if not to exonerate her, at least to elevate her crime to a higher ethical level than that of Oedipus. In contrast to Oedipus's crime, which is unconscious, Antigone's crime is conscious; as such it can be appropriated by Hegel to serve as an example of the necessary ethical conflict between the law of the state and the law of the family, all the more so since Antigone recognizes her error and, in so doing, the prominence of the state. However, even if Oedipus's crime is unconscious, it promotes the achievement of a conscious or tragic insight, whereas Antigone's crime, even though conscious, promotes the power of the unconscious, of the underground.

Taking Derrida's comment that Antigone suspends the

difference between the sexes one step further, I would suggest that, by taking action, Antigone subverts the sexual roles, blurs the boundaries between masculinity and femininity. As such, she creates havoc, disturbs the order of patriarchy and genealogy: hence her punishment is rightful, both for Sophocles and for Hegel. Her fate is in this regard similar to that of the poets in Plato's *Republic* and of Flora in Thomas Hall's *The Indictment of Flora*. In Hall's tract from 1661, the judge sums up the case against Flora as follows: 'Flora, thou hast been indicted for the bringing in abundance of misrule and disorder in to Church and State.'[7] Antigone, like the poets in Plato's *Republic*, and like flowers in texts, creates disorder in the state and in the text of Hegel by interfering with the rule of opposites. In *The Indictment of Flora*, the judgment is 'perpetual banishment.' The banishment is perpetual because, just as it is impossible to cut off the Hydra's heads (to castrate women) or to banish the poets, it is impossible to kill a flower or to entomb Antigone: flowers and poetry always return, albeit slightly metamorphosed, as the flowers of philosophic or juridical rhetoric, as the poetic speeches of Antigone return in Hegel's philosophical discourse. Through an unarrestable dissemination they persist, they creep in; they end up growing between the stones of the monumental elaboration that attempted to banish them.

This ubiquity & survival against all odds is what Hegel's strange fascination with Antigone illustrates. Indeed, even if Antigone is associated with death and burial – as flowers traditionally are – she also rises above death, which she denies and derides. Like the flower that falls on the ground so that another flower can be born in an eternal cycle of death and rebirth, Antigone must be sacrificed – it is her destiny and destination – so that the city of Thebes can eventually be regenerated.

In an article about the cultural and psychological relationship between flowers and death, Marie Bonaparte concludes that flowers, as symbols of the phallus, function as a denial of death: 'The flower also gets reborn each spring, like the phoenix, out of the ashes of the earth.'[8] Thus, Antigone's survival and descendancy – she herself is the progeny of incest – is not ensured through marriage in a genealogical and linear fashion but through metaphorical and poetic dissemination. She survives metaphorically in the text of Hegel, who, by letting her speak through his text, allows her to dictate her law, the nocturnal law of the unconscious which cannot be silenced.

This preliminary discussion reveals that the flower seems to have no *topos,* no clear or real place, no role. If flowers are traditionally – & as literary emblems, primordially – associated with feminine beauty, life, & innocence, they shift in the same texts into their opposite: they represent sin in Milton's *Paradise Lost;* in Baudelaire, they become the flowers of evil; in Genet, they are associated with criminals and homosexuals; in Proust, they suit both the description of the *jeunes filles en fleurs* and the decorum of homosexual attraction. Their actual morphology seems to invite this symbolic crossing of the genders: the receptacle-shaped corolla readily becomes a symbol of the womb, whereas the pistil with its erect style points to phallic symbolism. Remarking on this impossibility for the metaphor of the flower to remain in one particular and predetermined locus, Derrida shows in *Glas* that flowers seem to occupy instead the degree zero in the chain of signification. Involved as they are in the process of dissemination, flowers appear only to disappear, are present only as they metamorphose themselves endlessly into other things. It is in this sense that they are, as Bataille intimated, akin to the kind of substitutions at work in the unconscious.

The connections already alluded to between Bataille's and Hegel's assertions lead us to question the propriety or possibility of a 'language of flowers.' Instead of asking the traditional question (what do flowers express?), we should ask rather what motivates their appearance in texts, and what their appearance obscures. Rather than reading what the various flowers express, we should recognize the kinds of substitutions and translations they provoke. Rather than asking, like Bataille, about the linear and motivated relationship between the linguistic flower and its referent, we might explore what prompts their appearance in texts. In this respect, flowers, and their names, will be treated like any other signifiers, allowing us to pursue the obscured liaison between the feminine, the unconscious, and the text as a way of opening up the relationship between philosophy, literature, and psychoanalysis.

The botanical model of dissemination does not oppose signification or production (of meaning) but proposes an extravagant reading that reveals the act of writing as providing an excess of syntax over semantics, a waste, a squandering of seeds (& semes) out of which meaning is eventually gathered. The flower becomes the signifier par excellence, demonstrating the subsidiary roles to which the Western philosophical tradition based on truth, knowledge, and reason has relegated the flower, the feminine, the unconscious, the random, the nonlinear, sexuality, and, of course, the signifier in general. This relationship between flowers and the unconscious is unfolded in Freud's 'dream of the botanical monograph' and that of one of his patients, both appearing under the rubric of 'symbols in dreams' in *The Interpretation of Dreams*.

Freud uses his dream of the botanical monograph as an example of his theory of the displacement and distortion in dreams of some pressing unconscious material into some indifferent material from one's waking life. Here is Freud's record of his dream:

Ich habe eine Monographie über eine gewisse Pflanze geschrieben. Das Buch liegt vor mir, ich blättere eben eine eingeschlagene farbige Tafel um. Jedem Exemplar ist ein getrock-

*netes Spezimen der Pflanze beigebunden, ähnlich wie aus einem
Herbarium.*

*I had written a botanical monograph on a certain plant. The
book lay before me and I was at the moment turning over a
folded colored plate. Bound up in each copy was a dried up
specimen of the plant, as though it had been taken from a herbarium.*[9]

What is characteristic of Freud's report & interpretation of
his dream is the absence or exclusion of the flower in question. Indeed, Freud mentions that the unimportant, indifferent material of his waking life displaced in the dream is
precisely his seeing that very morning in a bookstore window a monograph, *The Genus Cyclamen*. In the interpretation of his dream, Freud insists that it was a monograph of
that plant, not of the flower. The indifferent flower does not
let itself be forgotten, however, as it becomes the absent
center of associations linked with forgetting. Thus Freud
tells us that cyclamens are his wife's favorite flowers, which
he often forgets to bring back for her; they remind him of
Frau L's story about her husband forgetting to bring her
flowers – an event that she interprets as a sign of his waning
desire; they also remind him of the name of one of his patients, Flora. Freud had recently used Frau L's story as 'Be-
weis für meine Behauptung . . . daßVergessen sehr haüfig
die Ausführung einer Absicht des Unbewußten sei und im-
merhin einen Schluß auf die geheime Gesinnung des Ver-
gessenden gestatte' (175) ['Evidence of my theory that forgetting is very often determined by an unconscious purpose and that it always enables one to deduce the secret
intentions of the person who forgets' (202)]. The flower
also seems to prompt the memory of a conversation Freud
had on the day of the dream with Herr Gärtner ('gardener')
and Dr. Königstein about Freud's monograph of another
plant, namely the coca plant. Freud's discovery of the properties of that plant as an anesthetic in eye operations was,

however, to be attributed to someone else, Dr. Koller. Freud remembers the conversation well enough not to have forgotten that he had complimented Frau Gärtner; she was *blooming (blühend)*, he had remarked. Did Frau Gärtner have a garden in her face, did her gardener-husband water her so often that she bloomed, or is she herself a flower, like Flora and Frau L? Or is it impossible to forget or repress the flower that always returns to haunt us, albeit in another guise?

Even though Freud uses this dream as an example of the displacement of indifferent material from one's waking life, he seems to be unaware of the displacements caused by his disregard of the flower. Thus, whereas in his patient's dream, Freud is interested in the particular flowers involved, their names, and possible symbolic meanings, here he seems to be oblivious to these 'indifferent' details. Freud's lack of regard for the flower is associated with seeing & nonseeing, recognition and nonrecognition, around which the dream revolves – with Freud in the role of both seer & nonseer. First, Freud does not see the flower for the plant; he does not see the flower as a flower, but sees that Frau Gärtner is blooming. Moreover, there are numerous references to seeing and eyes in the interpretation of this dream.

The references to eyes & seeing can be understood as being motivated by Freud's discovery of the use of cocaine as an anesthetic in eye operations; however, Freud's disregard of the flower in his own dream allows us to take the interpretation a step further, in a way that would explain Freud's self-reproaches. Freud's discovery of the use of cocaine in eye operations was not recognized because, as he tells us, 'ich war nicht gründlich genug, die Sache weiter zu verfolgen' (176) ['I had not been thorough enough to pursue the matter any further' (204)]. This, then, leads Freud to interpret his own dream as self-justification: 'Ich bin doch der Mann, der die wertvolle und erfogreiche Abhandlung ('über das Kokain) geschrieben hat' (179) ['After all, I am the man who wrote the valuable and memorable paper on cocaine' (206)]. The dream indeed revolves around the notion of recognition and nonrecognition, insight, the gift of seeing, aesthetics, and anesthetics, marked by Freud's ignorance of the flower & colors. Thus, there is a reference to Freud's father's eye operation where Freud's discovery was recognized by the anesthetist Dr. Koller. More interesting, however, is Freud's daydream about having glaucoma himself, going to Wilhelm Fliess's house in Berlin, and being operated on, incognito, by a surgeon recommended by Fliess. In Freud's daydream situation, the surgeon would talk about the benefits of cocaine in such operations, and Freud would not say anything about his share in the discovery. In this case, Freud would then be like the flower in his own dream, there but not there and ignored. Going to Fliess's house to recover vision is also telling, since Fliess, in this interpretation, is associated with long-range vision, with 'the gift of a seer.'

Associated with seeing & recognition are Freud's memories about his lack of interest in botany. Thus Freud tells us on the one hand about his passion for monographs, about his attraction to the 'colored plates' in medical books, but on the other about his failed attempt to draw one himself. Here again is the failure to see (the flower, the colors) and the consequent failure to be recognized. It is significant in this respect that the word *colored* appears so frequently in Freud's attempt to interpret the dream when color is practically absent in the actual report of the indifferent event that provoked the dream. Indeed, what emerges from Freud's report of the dream is neither the flower nor its color but 'a dried up specimen of the plant as if it had been taken out of a herbarium,' in other words, a flower having already become a sign, a flower in a book, very much like the 'botanical monograph' in *The Interpretation of Dreams*.

The childhood recollections brought about by this

dream all have to do with Freud's lack of interest in botany. Thus, the herbarium in the dream reminds Freud of a task assigned by his secondary school teacher of cleaning bookworms from the school's herbarium. Freud remembers that he had been given fewer sheets to clean up than other students. Similarly, in his preliminary examination, he had failed to identify the botanical species of the *crucifer*. The association between the plant & the book leads Freud to another childhood memory, which he deems 'das einzige, was mir aus dieser Lebenzeit in plastischer Erinnerung geblieben ist' (178) ['the only plastic memory of that period of my life' (205)]. Freud remembers that he and his sister had been given a book with colored plates to destroy. The action of tearing the book to pieces, leaf by leaf, was bound to remind Freud of a botanical analogue. Indeed, tearing off the petals of a daisy, as in the game of 'love me, love me not,' is a common amusement of children. However, this children's game does not bring up the metaphor of the daisy but of the artichoke, Freud's 'favorite flower.' The artichoke is known as a nonflowering plant, but the edible part of that plant is handled like a flower in the process of eating.

This transformation of the flower from a potential aesthetic object (the cyclamen) into an edible plant (the artichoke) establishes the link between the flower and the book, between the herbarium & the verbarium.[10] The association between the childhood memory of tearing a book to pieces & the process of eating an artichoke allows Freud to metamorphose into a bookworm, a detour through which he can express his conscious guilt about his expensive habit of collecting books, a displacement of his unconscious guilt about his inimical relationship to botany, not to mention probable worries about potency.

It should be noted that Freud criticizes the childhood game not in terms of aesthetics but in terms of its function: 'Its purpose was not very educational,' he remarks. Similarly, Freud's self-justification about his failure with botany is that 'es wäre mir schlecht ergangen, wenn nicht meine theoretische Kentnisse mir herausgeholfen hätten' (177) ['my prospects would not have been too *bright* if I had not been helped out by my theoretical knowledge' (204; my emphasis)].

One might well ask then what this dream has to do with flowers, and what the name and presence of the flower, the genus *Cyclamen,* hide. As I mentioned, it is significant that, contrary to his practice with regard to his patients' dreams of flowers, Freud does not analyze the particular flower. In the case of his patient's dream, two of the flowers involved are the violet & the carnation. In his interpretation, Freud reveals the relationship between the flowers, their names, and the unconscious thoughts hidden behind their appearance in the dream. Freud finds 'the dreamer's unconscious thoughts of the violence of defloration' inscribed within the name of the violet and the words *viola* and *violate,* with which it is related linguistically (380/410). The name 'carnation' leads Freud to acknowledge the relationship between the flower and repression. Thus, Freud's patient tries to repress the connection between the carnation and flesh, and says that she remembers the carnation for its color. The reference to flesh, which Freud's patient attempts to repress, Freud finds inscribed in the name of the flower. Indeed, *carnation* is derived from the Latin *carō,* meaning 'flesh,' but the word came to denote the color of flesh, a notion still inscribed in the word *incarnation* (380/410).

What then of the cyclamen, which Freud fails to analyze? In *The Poetry of Plants* (1907), Hugh Macmillan talks about 'the cyclamen of the Holy Land,' originating from Palestine, which he describes as follows: 'It looks like a prophet flower, with its ears bent back to hear the mystic voices of the past, looking to a future of restored glory.' Macmillan's impressionistic description, however, takes account of the shape of the cyclamen, which indeed appears as an inverted flower which, instead of blooming upward like a tulip, first turns its head down & then up. Macmillan's interest in the cyclamen is sparked by 'the mysterious markings on the leaves,' which he compares to 'some unknown cypher writing,' & in the red circles on the white petals.[11] As in Freud's dream, one sees here the association between flowers and writing, between flowers and the flowers of rhetoric, between the herbarium & the verbarium. Etymologically, the word *cyclamen* is derived from the Greek word *kuklos*, meaning 'circle,' or 'wheel,' and from the Indo-European root *kwel-*, which also developed into the Greek *tele*, meaning 'far.' In this respect, the cyclamen can be seen as linking past experiences with future ones, namely, Freud's past failures as well as his future glory, prophesied by Fliess, the one with the foresight of the cyclamen. Moreover, the Greek word *kuklos* and the word *cyclamen* allow us to see a division in the interpretation of the dream between the 'circle of women' (Frau Freud, Frau L, Flora, and Frau Gärtner), all associated with flowers, and the 'circle of men' (Dr. Freud, Dr. Königstein, and Dr. Koller), who use the flowers and plants for their theories. It should be noted also that ingestion of cyclamen is said to both purge the body and expel worms. As opposed to some wish-fulfilling dreams that Freud analyzes, this particular one definitely has a purging nature. The cyclamen, as the absent center of the dream, expels worms, especially bookworms, just as Freud's teacher had expelled bookworms from the school herbarium. In both cases, Freud is both the physical & psychological worm which makes the rose sick & makes Freud himself speak about the 'sorrows of passion.' In Freud's dream, and especially in the interpretation of his patient's dream, what strikes one is not so much the relationship between a particular flower and its symbolic meaning but a more deeply rooted association between the name of the flower and its appearance. The link between the flower and its meaning is therefore not a linear equivalence between signifier and signified, as in the classical conception of the language of flowers, but is instead unconscious and nonteleological.

Freud's interpretation of the flower as a dream element leads him intuitively, but against his will, to a conflicting point in his theory. Thus, it is significant that Freud interrupts this interpretation 'weil mich zur Mitteilung des Traums nur die Absicht bewogen hat, an einem Beispiele die Beziehung des Trauminhalts zu dem erregenden Erlebnis des Vortages zu untersuchen' (179) ['since my only purpose in reporting it was to illustrate by an example the relationship between the content of the dream and the experience of the previous day that provoked it' (206)]. It is obvious to the reader of Freud, and probably also to Freud himself, that, as an example of the linear and causal relationship between the dream content and the experience from waking life, the dream fails. The dream fails as an example precisely because the multiple meanings that Freud uncovers cannot be reduced to the unilateral meaning of the example. The botanical element of the dream, which Freud disregards – one could also say represses – sends Freud on the paths of dissemination, and the ramifications of these meanings are in conflict with his desire to elaborate psychoanalytic theory into a science, into knowledge. Freud, therefore, has to interrupt the analysis and opt for mastery and unity over the plurality of meanings which would jeopardize his enterprise and lead him to acknowledge the random, the nonlinear, which the botanical element conveys and which Freud himself acknowledges elsewhere in *The Interpretation of Dreams*:

In den bestgedeuteten Traümen muß man oft eine Stelle im Dunkel lassen, weil man bei der Deutung merkt, daß dort ein Knäuel von Traumgedanken anhebt, der sich nicht entwirren will, aber auch zum Trauminhalt keine weiteren Beiträge geliefert hat. Dies ist dann der Nabel des Traums, die Stelle an der dem Unerkannten aufsitzt. Die Traumgedanken, auf die man bei der Deutung gerät, müssen ja ganz allgemein ohne

Abschluß bleiben und nach allen Seiten hin in die netzartige Verstrickung unserer Gedankenwelt auslaufen. Aus einer dichteren Stelle dieses Geschlechts erhebt sich dann der Traumwunsch wie der Pilz aus einem Mycelium. (530)

There is often a passage in even the most thoroughly interpreted dream which has to be left obscure; this is because we become aware during the work of interpretation that at that point there is a tangle of dream-thoughts which cannot be unravelled and which moreover adds nothing to our knowledge of the content of the dream. This is the dream's navel, the spot where it reaches down into the unknown. The dream-thoughts to which we are led by interpretation cannot, from the nature of things, have definite endings; they are bound to branch out in every direction into the intricate network of our world of thought. It is at some point where this meshwork is particularly close that the dream-wish grows up, like a mushroom out of a mycelium. (564)

When Freud acknowledges, as in this passage, the endlessness of psychoanalytic interpretation of dreams, and recognizes their nonlogocentric nature, he falls onto organic metaphors and on the rhizomatic root system akin to the model developed by Deleuze and Guattari, which I discuss later. Moreover, Freud's choice of words in this passage leads him unwittingly to emphasize the relationship between the organic, the unconscious, and the underworld. In this respect, Freud's disregard of the flower in his dream and his reproaches about his lack of interest in botany become meaningful and can be read as a symptom of Freud's conflicting views of the unconscious. Freud's guilt is his recognition of his rejection of the botanical model which would liberate the unconscious in favor of the logocentric model at work in the elaboration of any scientific specialization, inevitably marked by mastery, exclusion, silencing, and repression.

In *Glas*, Derrida shows the reductionist nature of the

classical reading which attempts to confine the flower within a systemic equivalence of signifier and signified. For Derrida, the nonteleological relationship between signifier & signified exemplified in the flower deconstructs Freud's opting for mastery, exclusion, and repression: 'La destruction pratique de l'effet transcendantal est à l'oeuvre dans la structure de la fleur, comme de toute *partie* en tant qu'elle *apparaît* ou pousse *comme telle*' (GL 21–22b) ['The practical deconstruction of the transcendental effect is at work in the structure of the flower as of every *part* inasmuch as *it appears* or grows (*pousse*) *as such*' (GL 15b)]. Indeed, the flower is both part and whole, as well as part for the whole, scientifically and metaphorically. Derrida tells us that 'la fleur est partie,' because it is a part, part for the whole, but also departed, as it is made to signify univocally as either ornament or example. Caught in the system of symbolization, the flower as lively multiplicity disappears into the unity & stability of the signified. This is why Derrida quotes Genet: 'Elles ne symbolisaient rien' (GL 57b) ['They (the flowers) symbolized nothing' (GL 47b)]: the flower cannot symbolize anything, as it is already, and at the origin, part of an originless chain of signification linked to the process of dissemination.

In the same demonstration, Derrida claims that flowers cannot symbolize anything because of the process of metamorphosis in which they are involved. Thus, like gloves and shoes (fetishes), flowers can always be turned inside out into their opposite: 'Pour que la castration recoupe la virginité, le phallus se renverse en vagin, les opposés prétendus s'équivalent et se réfléchissent, il faut que la fleur se retourne comme un gant, et son style comme une gaine' (GL 57b) ['For castration to overlap virginity, for the phallus to be reversed into the vagina, for alleged opposites to be equivalent to each other and reflect each other, the flower has to be turned inside out like a glove and its style like a sheath' (GL 47b)]. Like the fetish, the flower is detachable, cuttable, *coupable* in French, as in Derrida's text, therefore both cuttable and culpable, and as such part of an economy that reconciles contraries. Like the fetish, the flower allows an oscillation between contraries, between feminine and masculine, between phallus and vagina, between 'pénis/vagin, castration/virginité, érection/retombée, organisme naturel/artefact désarticulé, corps propre total/morceau fétichisé, etc. (GL 144b) ['penis/vagina, castration/virginity, erection/relapse, natural organism/disarticulated artifact, total body proper/fetishized morsel' (GL 126b)]. It is in this respect that the flower appears as the site of the deconstruction of the transcendental effect & can serve as a disseminative agency for Derrida's deconstruction of hermeneutic or psychoanalytic interpretation. The flower, which in *Glas* is always a funerary flower, opens a gap in the system of signification as it refuses to be reduced to any mimetic representation relying on an equivalence between the word and the thing.

As in the analysis of Freud's flower dreams, flowers in discourse are related to the work of the unconscious. Rather than referring to a reality outside themselves (like real flowers), they reveal the work of repression. As such, they confuse the opposition between motivation & arbitrariness, or, more precisely, they reveal the work of the unconscious in motivation and vice versa. Moreover, as Derrida's *Glas* & Freud's interpretation of his own dream and of his patient's point out, there are relationships between flowers, the textile, and the textual. Thus, significantly, in both interpretations of flower dreams, Freud does not rely on botany for analysis, as might have been expected, but on literary texts, on texts in which flowers appear. Thus, Freud's patient's memory of camellias brings up Freud's reference to *La Dame aux camélias,* as well as Goethe's poem 'Die Müllerins Verrat.' Similarly, in a consequent attempt to come to terms with the content and the mechanics of his own dream, Freud falls upon two significant literary examples. In his attempt to defend his interpretation (which, as he himself recognizes, 'can be attacked on the ground of being *arbitrary* and artificial' (209; my emphasis) and the ensuing theory of condensation and distortion occurring in dreams, Freud refers to Othello's handkerchief and quotes Goethe.

The example of Othello's handkerchief is used to explain how 'ideas which originally had only a weak charge of intensity' (the botanical monograph in Freud's dream) 'take over the charge from ideas which were originally intensely cathected' (the lack of recognition of Freud for the discovery of the properties of cocaine, or his disregard for botany). The reference, and quotation from Goethe's *Faust,* combines even more clearly the botanical, the textile, and the textual, which Derrida develops in *Glas.* To explain the combinations converging upon the nodal point of the 'botanical' monograph, Freud remarks, 'Here we find ourselves in a factory of thoughts where, as in "the weaver's masterpiece" –

A thousand threads one needle throws,
Where fly the shuttle hither and thither,
Unseen the threads are knit together,
And an infinite combination grows. (317)

It is significant that Freud would fall upon a quotation from Goethe, who also wrote a botanical work on the metamorphosis of plants, to explain the combinations (in this case brought about by the presence of plants) and transformations characteristic of dreams. Here we find expressed unconsciously the link between the appearance of flowers in texts and the kind of metamorphoses and translations to which they subject any text.

Derrida uses the link between flowers and the unconscious to retrieve Genet's discourse from the reductive and judgmental hermeneutic enterprises of Jean Paul Sartre's and Bataille's interpretations. Leaning on Genet's name –

the name of a flower – Derrida translates the concept of *vol* from Genet's discourse not as 'theft' as Sartre does but as 'flight,' which he sees as more befitting Genet's flowery discourse. Using the discourse of botany, Derrida reads Genet's texts by taking into account the appearance of flowers. Since Genet's name, his mother's name, happens to be the name of a flower (genêt, *Genista*), albeit with a slight graphic difference, it is difficult when one reads him not to be struck by the scattered references to the broom flower and its properties, as well as by the presence of a whole flowery discourse animating his narratives.

What strikes one immediately about the broom flower is how closely it is linked to metamorphosis – physical and linguistic, as well as heraldic. As a name, it is significant that the *Genista* is associated with the idea of the crossing of borders and with translation. Indigenous to England, where it derived its name from one of its functions & variations (broom, basam, bisom, bizzom, browne, breeam, etc.), the botanical description of the plant resembles a catalog that seems to announce the disseminative discourse of Genet, Derrida's plays on words, and the kinds of linguistic transformations at work in James Joyce's *Finnegans Wake*. Moreover, botanists note that 'broom' is also related etymologically to the Germanic word *brōm* meaning 'to sweep.' More significantly, it was adopted as a badge of Brittany and by the dynasty of the Plantagenets (*Planta Genista*). Most herbals thus quote Geoffrey of Anjou when he adopted the plant as his emblem: 'This golden plant, rooted firmly amid the rock, yet upholding what is ready to fall, shall be my cognizance.' Besides, we find out that the *Colle à Genet*, the collar of a special order created by St. Louis, bore the motto: 'Exaltat humiles' (He exalts the lowly).[12] Genet's gesture of comparing criminals to flowers is similar to the motto with which the genêt flower has been associated, namely to elevate the lowly, to give the *criminels de droit commun*, a right to a name.

In *The Savage Mind* (*La Pensée Sauvage* – not only 'Wild Thought[s]' but also homophonically 'Wild Pansies'), Lévi-Strauss comments on the see-saw movement (*chassé-croisé*), between proper names and the names of flowers. We give flowers the names of people, but once they have become the names of flowers, we give them back to people.[13] Such a see-saw movement is perceptible here. What is noteworthy is that the broom flower seems to be associated with naming: it named a dynasty and Genet, and thereby gave kings and poets the prerogative of naming.

The very nature of the broom flower is also buried within the economy of Genet's text: the economy of botany can thus be seen in direct opposition to the kind of economy expressed by ontological models. Within the natural world of flowers, as in Genet's life and discourse, there is a randomness and waste, which runs counter to the teleology of the Hegelian model. This randomness is also related to the metamorphoses and unrepresentational mimicries and uncertainties associated with flowers as well as with the (criminal) characters in Genet's novels. If Genet can identify the criminals/homosexuals in his novels with flowers, it might mean that the flowers are not as innocent as Hegel might have supposed, or as indifferent. Indeed, the flowers are not innocent in the Hegelian scheme; they are rather the flowers of evil, because they fall outside the boundaries of Absolute Knowledge and the law of the state. The world of flowers is, like that of Genet's novels, a world where things are not necessarily what they seem to be: flowers look like butterflies, seduce insects, mimic them, are violated by them. Similarly, in Genet's novels, criminals are saints and virgins, homosexuals are neither men nor women.

It should then be no surprise if Derrida is interested in the botanical discourse or in the world of plants, from which he had already borrowed the term *dissemination*. The word 'dissemination' implies that meaning does not happen in a linear and teleological fashion but according to an alliance of rule and chance. Production of meaning, or survival of the species, happens in the botanical or linguistic world through a scattering of seeds or semes. Thus in the world of flowers, reproduction, survival, fecundation is the rule; yet this *telos* is achieved through chance and intermediaries (insects, water, air, animals, humans).

In *Les Plantes: Amours et civilisations végétales,* Jean-Marie Pelt uses the metaphor of the postal service to explain the work of pollination and fecundation. One can see Derrida's evident attraction to this system of production, which does not rely on a stable subject at the origin of a message that is never assured of arriving at its destination. In Derrida's work, as in the botanical system, the destination, the life, the product are a result of the sorting out (*le triage postal*) at the destination; it is the *destinataire* (recipient of the letter) who eventually gives meaning to the writing process, who countersigns the act of writing. Thus, in his comparison between the game of reproduction and the postal system, Jean-Marie Pelt wants to establish the alliance in botanical reproduction between rule and chance. There is a purpose, 'amener le pollen sur le stigmate de l'ovaire et réussir ainsi la fécondation' [to bring the pollen to the stigma of the ovary and thus achieve fecundation]. For that purpose to be achieved, however, the flower has to rely on intermediaries and chance.

On fait confiance au transporteur et au hasard: il finira toujours par arriver quelque chose à destination, à condition d'en expédier beaucoup. Qu'importe alors si des sacs entiers, des sacs de pollen s'entend, ne sont jamais livrés et n'arrivent jamais à destination. Dans l'oeuvre de la pollinisation, la nature n'est pas regardante: elle se fie au hasard, néglige, gaspille.

One thus trusts the carrier and chance: something will always eventually reach its destination, provided a lot is sent. What does it matter if whole bags – bags of pollen, that is – are never delivered, never reach their destination. In the work of pol-lination, nature is not particular; it trusts chance, neglects, squanders.[14]

Moreover, in this scheme, it is neither the auxiliary in the work of production nor the sending subject that is in control and does the sorting out (*le triage*) but the *destinataire*, the stigma. Fecundation, or production of meaning, is thus established at the destination. But nothing is ever as simple as that, either in the world of nature or in the world of texts. There is no simple randomness but always a complex recognition on the part of the receiver (*destinataire*) of the origin of the pollen (or message).

Here again, we notice the transformation of the flower into the letter, the transformation of the herbarium into the verbarium. The reader, as stigma of the flower, is the one who ensures the signature and life of the writer, as flower. The writer is the one at risk, the seducer of intermediaries who has to rely on wind and chance so that his or her message reaches its destination, all the while knowing that it always will reach its destination, albeit through many detours.

My purpose in this procession or anthology involving a scattering of the names of Bataille, Hegel, Freud, Genet, Derrida, and a few botanists has been to bring to the fore the effects of the appearance of flowers in texts. Returning to Freud, albeit taking his words out of the context of the conscious elaboration of psychoanalysis into a separate scientific discipline, one could argue that the presence of flowers in discourse, whether classical or modernist, points to a *topos* in texts which defies hermeneutic expertise. It would seem that, rather than letting themselves complacently be reduced to the secondary status of symbols or examples that would obscure their specificity and plurality, flowers point to a degree zero of interpretation; they deconstruct the effect of the transcendental signified. Even though, as discursive and literary devices, they seem to have little left to do with the botanical world out of which they stem and which they only vaguely seem to recall, they offer an alternative model of the production (of meaning) which would take into account what has been rejected and repressed in logocentric systems of thought and knowledge, namely plurality, the feminine, the unconscious, and the signifier.

The relationship between the herbarium and the verbarium I have delineated here is not new; it is, on the contrary, part of a long, but forgotten, tradition in which botany and literature are linked, as the humanities and the sciences once were in our academic institutions. Keeping this affinity in mind, it is not so surprising to find that most botanical works that deserve the consecrated qualification of science make frequent allusions to linguistics, poetry, and myth, or that major literary figures such as Rousseau, Goethe, and Ruskin devoted their time to their minor passion and wrote botanical works, mostly ignored in literary circles.[15] Even if, like Rousseau's 'Lettres sur la botanique,' they gave these writers the illusion that botany was a natural refuge from the artificiality of literature, these works unconsciously stress the close relationship between the linguistic and the botanical. If one wonders why these two domains cross so readily, one simply has to look at our common metaphors and games: we talk about the 'roots' and 'stems' of words, the 'flowers of rhetoric'; we use flowers and tea leaves to tell our stories; while botanists derive the names of some flowers from the myths recorded in Ovid's *Metamorphoses* and find the properties of plants in what they call 'the doctrine of signatures.'[16]

Modernist and postmodernist writers, such as Proust, Rilke, Genet, Cixous, and Ponge – to name only a few, if they do not write botanical treatises like Rousseau, Goethe, and Ruskin had done before them, nevertheless owe the inspiration of some of their most beautiful pages to a reading of and personal affinity with that science. Thus, it might not be well known that Proust borrowed the description of the sexual attraction between Jupien and the Baron de Charlus from Charles Darwin's *The Various Contrivances by which Orchids Are Fertilized by Insects* (discussed in chapter 2).

In the world of critical theory, Jacques Derrida's work (especially *La Dissémination* and *Glas*) and Gilles Deleuze and Felix Guattari's *Mille Plateaux* (especially the chapter entitled 'Le Rhyzome') recover this lost tradition and emphasize the correspondence between the mode of production in the vegetable world and in the work of art (see chapter 2). Recovering the botanical model of signification allows one both to save the reading of texts from genealogical and linear translations and to give free rein to the forces of the unconscious, which are necessarily involved in any writing or reading.

If we are serious when we talk about the life of a work of art, we might acknowledge the complexity & mystery of life & of the work of art rather than reducing them through our ready-made concepts and categories. We might learn from natural scientist Jean-Marie Pelt, who, after discussing the 'amours et civilizations' of plants, concludes, 'La vie est toujours plus complexe que nous le croyons. Elle a horreur de se laisser enfermer dans nos concepts et garde toujours une large part de potentialités non-exprimées, d'initiatives possibles, voire de fantaisies inattendues' [Life is always more complex than we think. It abhors letting itself be imprisoned within our concepts and always keeps a large part of non-expressed potentialities, of possible initiatives, of unexpected games].[17] We might ponder with Marcel in *A la recherche du temps perdu,* who, after observing the double, miraculous encounter between the orchid and the wasp and between Jupien and the Baron de Charlus, muses, 'J'avais déjà tiré de la ruse apparente des fleurs une conséquence sur toute une partie inconsciente de l'oeuvre littéraire' ['I had already drawn from the visible stratagems of flowers a conclusion that bore upon a whole unconscious element of literary production'].[18] Or we might want to follow Alice, who, after contemplating making a daisy chain, encounters a white rabbit with pink eyes and penetrates a wonderland of linguistic metamorphoses where things never seem to be what they are and where the key principles and rules learned at school no longer open any door.

CHAPTER TWO

Writing from the Underworld

Proust and Rilke

I have been into the bowels of old Mother Earth, and seen wonders and learnt much curious knowledge in the regions of darkness. – Charles Darwin

Attempting to define the flower seems to have presented an insurmountable challenge to natural scientists in all periods. In his 'Lettres sur la botanique,' Rousseau mentions the first problem, namely to differentiate between the 'literary' flower, the flower of rhetoric, & the 'natural' flower, the object of scientific investigation (chapter 1). As Derrida demonstrates in 'La Mythologie blanche,' the distinction between the proper & the figurative is untenable, especially in the case of the flower which, especially when cut, always runs the risk of becoming a metaphor. Indeed, we have seen, with Bataille, for instance, how the flower disappears as such when it is used to emblematize human characteristics: where one might have 'seen' a rose, one now sees 'love,' where one might have seen a lily, one sees the paradox of phallic 'virginity.' Of course the flower, especially through the presence of the definite article, is already a metaphor, because its materiality and naturalness have been effaced by conceptual significance. Each time the definite article is used, the flower is already cut from the realm of nature to be raised to that of concept. And when the flower is cut, its destiny and destination are all too clear: it inevitably ends up in the pages of a book.

If the same could be said almost of any word having a specific referent, and if it is true that the use of the definite article has that effect on any common noun, the flower, because it is cuttable (*coupable*) seems to be more readily culpable (*coupable*) of that fall into language. For to appreciate a flower is to cut it, and to cut a flower is to cite it. In 'La Mythologie blanche,' Derrida concludes his discussion of metaphor with the following passage:

Telle fleur porte toujours son double en elle-même, que ce soit la graine ou le type, le hasard de son programme ou la nécessité de son diagramme. L'héliotrope peut toujours se relever. Elle peut toujours devenir une fleur sechée dans un livre. Il y a toujours absente de tout jardin, une fleur sechée dans un livre; et en raison de la répétition où elle s'abîme sans fin, aucun langage ne peut réduire en soi la structure d'une anthologie. Ce supplément du code qui traverse son champ, en déplace sans cesse la clôture, brouille la ligne, ouvre le cercle, aucune ontologie n'aura pu la réduire.

Such a flower always bears its double within itself, whether it be seed or type, the chance of its program or the necessity of its diagram. The heliotrope can always be relevé *[sublated]. And it can always become a dried flower in a book. There is always, absent from every garden, a dried flower in a book; and by virtue of the repetition in which it endlessly puts itself into* abyme, *no language can reduce into itself the structure of an anthology. This supplement of a code which traverses its own field, endlessly displaces its closure, breaks its line, opens its circle, and no ontology will have been able to reduce it.*[1]

Rousseau's struggle to define the flower dramatizes this see-saw between the 'natural' and the 'metaphorical' – a seesaw that unsettles the oppositions Rousseau would like to maintain between the two categories. From the flower in nature to the flower of rhetoric, there is only one short step, which Rousseau inevitably takes when, to explain the impossibility of defining the flower, he cites Augustine: 'Quand je me demande ce que c'est le temps . . . je le sais fort bien; je ne le sais plus quand on me le demande' [When I ask myself what time is . . . I know, but I no longer know when I am asked]. And Rousseau adds, 'On en pourrait dire la même chose de la fleur et peut-être même de la beauté, qui comme elle est la rapide proie du temps' [The same could be said of the flower, and perhaps of beauty which, like the flower, is a prey to time].[2] It is not by chance that the associations that come to Rousseau's mind happen to be the two concepts conventionally and metaphorically attributed to the flower and even 'defined' by it. And when Rousseau eventually 'defines' the flower, the flower becomes a metaphor for ephemeral beauty: the flower is a flower from the time its corolla opens till the time it fades. During that time it is literally an embodiment, a making visible, of the passage of time, and as such it is a metaphor for transience, temporality, and pathos. Moreover, the flower depends for its existence and denomination on the eye of the observer able to see its passage from opening to fading, from presence to absence. For the flower is meant to be seen, all the more so for its transience. Rousseau emphasizes this point, and so does Ruskin whose studies on plants grew out of the volumes of his *Modern Painters*.

Although their views differ, one finds in both Rousseau and Ruskin the same privileging of human – and thus reasoned – vision. In 'Proserpina,' his major work on plants, Ruskin argues that 'the flower exists for its own sake, not for the fruit's sake,' the fruit being just an added honor, a consolation for its death: 'The flower is the end of the seed, not the seed of the flower. . . . The glory is in being – not in begetting.'[3] Further criticizing botanists, such as Erasmus Darwin, who considered that flowers were beautiful so that they could attract insects, Ruskin argues, 'All these materialisms, in their unclean stupidity, are essentially the work of human bats, men of semi-faculty or semi-education, who are more or less incapable of so much as seeing' (263). When Ruskin finally asks, 'Do you think that flowers were born to nourish the blind?' (250), we realize that, moving from one teleology to another, but always on a straight line, flowers seem to be there, certainly not for their own sake, but for the sole purpose of being contemplated by educated artistic souls. They might as well be paintings or 'stained glass windows,' as Ruskin's favorite analogy has it. In this case it is the opposition between natural & artificial realms of significance that the flower has a tendency to unsettle.

In *The Origin of Species,* Charles Darwin refutes this kind of anthropocentrism, and argues that flowers have beautiful colors so that they can be observed by insects and thus be pollinated: 'When a flower is fertilized by the wind, it never has a gaily coloured corolla. Several plants habitually produce two kinds of flowers; one kind open and coloured, so as to attract insects, the other closed, not coloured, destitute of nectar, and never visited by insects.'[4] Under the disguise of scientific reasoning based on observation lurks a strange breed of anthropocentrism and cultural judgment. We may ask what 'a gaily coloured corolla' is and in whose eyes? Here, it seems that it is in the eyes of insects, but it hardly matters: whether for the eye of humans, or for that of insects, flowers cannot be beautiful for themselves, or for the wind. We have to hope that insects see the way we do. And we may wonder what happens to the 'beautiful' anemone or wind-flower in this reasoned vision, since it is folly to want to seduce the wind. In the absence of myth, there might be many absences in the gardens of science.

What strikes one in all these 'scientific' discussions is the exclusion of the other senses with which the flower could naturally be associated, namely smell and touch, and even the ear, as we shall see. In *Les Mots et les choses,* Michel Foucault discusses, in his chapter on natural history in the eighteenth century, this 'privilège presqu'exclusif de la vue' ['this almost exclusive privilege of vision']:

Observer, c'est donc se contenter de voir. De voir systématique-ment peu de chose. De voir ce qui, dans la richesse un peu confuse de la représentation, peut s'analyser, être reconnu par tous et recevoir un nom que chacun pourra entendre.

To observe, then, is to be content with seeing – with seeing few things systematically, with seeing what, in the rather confused wealth of representation, can be analyzed, recognized by all, and thus given a name that everyone will be able to under-stand.[5]

This description of scientific observation in the eighteenth century – which still applies now – depends on a vision whose purpose is to classify, put in categories, set limits, separate subject (as observer) from object (as observed), and thus conveniently establish a language based on the repetition of the same, which alone allows communication.

All systems of thought that privilege vision derive their authority from the Apollonian light of the sun, reason, male law, while they always repress the Dionysian play of sound, the unconscious, the multiple, and the feminine. As op-posed to this diurnal model, the 'floral' model of signifi-cation that I have developed reintroduces what has been excluded: darkness, the underworld, the unconscious. The flower, which has its roots in the underground, always leads back to it. In this way, it reminds us of the polymor-phic and dynamic life that is buried under the name it re-ceives by enlightened vision. Discussing Hegel's 'philoso-phy of nature' in *Glas,* Derrida uncovers the motives be-hind this kind of domination.

Tel est le 'concept de la philosophie de la nature': la libération du concept qui veut se rassembler auprès de lui-même après

avoir organisé le suicide de la nature, c'est-à-dire de son dou-
ble, de son 'miroir' (Spiegel) et de son 'reflet' (Reflex). Celui-ci
le captait mais le dispersait aussi dans son image, dans son
sorte de polymorphie qu'il fallait réduire. Il fallait strictement
assujettir le Protée (diesen Proteus zu bezwingen). (GL,
134a)

Such is the 'concept of the philosophy of nature': the setting free
of the concept that wants to reassemble itself close by itself
after having organized the suicide of nature, that is, of its dou-
ble, of its 'mirror' (Spiegel), of its 'reflection' (Reflex). The
reflection captured the concept but also dispersed it in its im-
age, in a kind of polymorphism that had to be reduced. The
Proteus had strictly to be subjugated (diesen Proteus zu bez-
wingen). (GL 117a)

Subjection or domination is always attempted of what is
dangerous, subversive, varied: in time it has been writing,
the body, woman, nature, the unconscious. We shall see
what these terms have in common, & the common repression that their exclusion hides. Writing from the underworld then will imply a return to a mythic unity between
human beings & the universe, a unity that the flowers –
especially in their association with the underworld – indicate. Thus, while it appears that the emergence of flowers in
texts points to an obscure 'nodal' point in the text which
resists hermeneutic analysis, their appearance also seems
motivated by the writer's desire to repair the Cartesian division of body and mind, subject and object, inside and outside. As a result this model of signification appeals to those
modernist and postmodernist writers who, either themat-
ically or conceptually, oppose the mimetic, logocentric, &
patriarchal order of the world. As the issue and agent of dissemination, flowers point, on the one hand, to the disseminative – rather than the centered – nature of linguistic production, and on the other, to our own scattering by the
forces of language.

Thus, in *A la recherche du temps perdu*, Marcel's task as an artist is not so much to recapture or recollect lost time but, as Georges Poulet has noted, to recapture lost space, that is, to re-collect, to gather together again the lost portions of self scattered through the process of living and seeing.[6] To write of the self is to read it, to gather it, as Proust, Heidegger, and the Greek verb *legein* (to gather, to read) suggest. It seems that in Proust's world, there is a reciprocal relationship between the seer and the seen. In observing, the self retains a particle of the observed object just as the observed object retains a particle of the observing self. The self itself is here neither unique nor stable but rather always involved in a natural disseminative process. The task of the artist will thus be to recollect those scattered particles of self, and in the process re-create the world.[7] Thus, in 'Le Temps retrouvé,' Marcel describes the creation of the work of art as going in the opposite direction of life, as undoing the work of life, in the same way that Penelope unravels at night what she weaves by day, in the same way that the flower which is born at day seems to die at night.[8]

Ce travail qu'avaient fait notre amour-propre, notre passion, notre esprit d'imitation, notre intelligence abstraite, nos habitudes, c'est le travail que l'art défera, c'est la marche en sens contraire, le retour aux profondeurs où ce qui a existé réellement gît inconnu de nous, qu'il nous fera suivre. (3:896)

Our vanity, our passions, our spirit of imitation, our abstract intelligence, our habits have long been at work, and it is the task of art to undo this work of theirs, making us travel back in the direction from which we have come to the depths where what has really existed lies unknown within us. (3:932)

To Marcel, the work of art is a quest for truth; however, this quest is not the Platonic quest for the ideal form behind the world of appearances, but rather the quest for the authentic unbounded self underneath the material and historical existence of everyday life. This quest for truth through art is therefore, as Jacques Lacan has understood, an Orphic descent into the underworlds of sleep, the unconscious, and the flower. This recollection of the unity of the self, this remembrance is, however, impossible to achieve if by unity one means the reconstitution of the One as Singularity. If the Orphic myth is going to serve as a model of the artist's recollection of the buried remnants of the artist's past, one has to realize that the past, the lost Eurydice, cannot be recovered through the agency of the will. The descent into the underworld rather happens on its own terms, that is, as a kind of apprenticeship to another kind of reality, a world where the borderlines between self and other, inside and outside, masculine and feminine disappear. In short, a reality where all oppositions fall together, where everything merges into something else, as happens in dreams.

In *Allegories of Reading,* Paul de Man writes that *A la recherche* 'narrates the flight of meaning.'[9] Criticism of Proust has for decades tried to establish the unity, the center of *A la recherche,* to turn the work into a conscious enterprise leading to a definition of the work of art. This kind of idealized notion of the work of art seems as remote as can be from Proust's world, where, as de Man points out, meaning depends almost entirely on a process of flight or dissemination. We might remind ourselves that *A la recherche* significantly starts when Marcel falls asleep. In the darkness of his bedroom, between sleep and wakefulness, he asks himself whether the light is on or off; whether he is awake or dreaming that he is awake. From this point through the million and a half words that follow, Marcel's self is in flight. This realm between sleeping and waking that inaugurates *A la recherche* allows us to read Marcel's apprenticeship as a descent into the world of the unconscious, a descent that enables him to understand the floral birth of the work of art.

The two things that Marcel seems to have learned at the end of 'Le Temps retrouvé' – right before he is supposed to write – is the role of the nocturnal muse which 'binds together' things that appeared separated in the world of light, and the role of chance (*le hasard*) in the production of the work of art. Hence, when Proust talks about the work of art as the presentation of truth, that truth revealed in art can only manifest itself as a metaphor – and metaphor is also a 'turning away.' Truth is but a moment in this folding and unfolding, this revealing and concealing. Proust's conception of the metaphor is not that of identification, or mirroring of one thing into another. Rather, it is the dynamic relationship and encounter between two discrete things, the copulation between contraries out of which emerges a harmony which preserves difference:

On peut faire se succéder indéfiniment dans une description les objets qui figuraient dans un lieu décrit, la vérité ne commencera qu'au moment où l'écrivain prendra deux objets différents, posera leur rapport analogue dans le monde de l'art à celui qu'est le rapport unique de la loi causale dans le monde de la science, et les enfermera dans les anneaux nécessaires d'un beau style; même, ainsi que la vie, quand, en rapprochant une qualité commune à deux sensations, il dégagera leur essence commune en les réunissant l'une et l'autre pour les soustraire aux contingences du temps, dans une métaphore. La nature . . . n'était-elle pas commencement d'art elle-même, elle qui ne m'avait permis de connaître, souvent, la beauté d'une chose que dans une autre. (3:889)

He can describe a scene by describing one after another the innumerable objects which at a given moment were present in a particular place, but truth will be attained by him only when he takes two different objects, states the connexion between them – a connexion analogous in the world of art to the unique connexion which in the world of science is provided by the law of causality – and encloses them in the necessary links of a well-wrought style; truth – and life too – can be attained by us only when, by comparing a quality common to two sensations,

we succeed in extracting their common essence & in reuniting
them to each other, liberated from the contingencies of time,
within a metaphor. Nature . . . was she not herself a beginning
of art, she who, often, had allowed me to become aware of the
beauty of one thing only in another thing. (3:924–25)

This connection between two objects or two sensations in a
metaphor does not rely on identity or adequation; on the
contrary, it is rather the kind of connection that Deleuze
and Guattari describe as 'rhyzomatic,' that is, the kind of
relationship in which 'il n'y a pas ni imitation ni ressem-
blance, mais explosion de deux series hétérogènes dans la
ligne de fuite composée d'un rhizome commun qui ne peut
plus être attribué, ni soumis à quoi que ce soit de signifiant'
['there is neither imitation, nor resemblance, only an ex-
ploding of two heterogeneous series on the line of flight
composed by a common rhyzome that can no longer be
attributed to or subjugated by anything signifying']. It is
indeed through this reciprocal relationship between the
world and the mind of the artist that the work of art can
appear as truth. To describe this reciprocal relationship,
this process of writing, Deleuze and Guattari use the relationship between the orchid and the wasp, which they define as 'un véritable devenir, un devenir-guêpe de l'orchidée
et un devenir-orchidée de la guêpe' ['a veritable becoming,
a becoming-wasp of the orchid and a becoming-orchid of
the wasp'].[10]

Significantly, it is through watching the encounter, and
possible fertilization, of a bee and a rare orchid – a story
already told by Charles Darwin – that Marcel understands
the codes of homosexual decorum, but more important, he
learns from the ruses of flowers the part played by the unconscious in the production of the work of art. The whole
passage enacts a descent into the underworld of Marcel's
unconscious in which Marcel becomes a botanist and, in
turn, Darwin's orchid and bee become metamorphosed into
Charlus and Jupien, and Proust's Charlus and Jupien be-

come metamorphosed into an orchid and a bee. One should be reminded here not only of the kind of transformations that occur in dreams but also of the metamorphoses that occur in the myths of the Underworld – as in Ovid's *Metamorphoses* or Lewis Carroll's *Alice in Wonderland* where humans turn into flowers, where playing cards turn into flowers, and flowers talk. As always, the descent is an apprenticeship into a mode of production that does not rely on the stability of reason or the work of intentionality, but rather depends on the forces of the unconscious. Like Alice, Marcel is here struck by unforeseen modes of signification that make him doubt the eye as the arbiter of truth.

The long passage detailing the encounter between Charlus & Jupien is momentous in *A la recherche* because it allows Marcel finally to understand what he had attempted to learn from flowers in his youth. The mere number of passages which describe Marcel's fascination with flowers, and all the references to the world of plants (and to botanical laws) scattered in Proust's text, seem to suggest that Marcel is supposed to learn something important from them, some secret that they do not hide from him, but which he cannot willfully grasp. Marcel's study of life in the salons and his contemplation of flowers are two aspects of the same passion – each helping to understand the other, till the opposition between nature and culture leads to a rapprochement. As such the flowers seem to reconcile the contraries that Marcel's conscious mind had kept separate. Hence their association with sleep, dream, the unconscious, where contraries also merge freely.

Marcel's first encounter with hawthorns is not in their natural environment, but in a church. As such they blend with the saintly but festive characteristics of their external environment. Marcel seems to be able to see the flowers only in their culturally determined meaning. As such, they simply mirror the environment in which they have been placed, and it is the environment that lends them their characteristics. They appear to Marcel as 'inséparables des mystères de la célébration' (1:112) ['inseparable from the mysteries in whose celebration they participated' (1:121)], they make him think of the ornaments on a bridal train. On the flowers, Marcel notices 'de petites places plus blondes sous lesquelles je me figurai que devait être cachée cette odeur, comme, sous les parties gratinées, le goût d'une frangipane où, sous leurs taches de rousseur, celui des joues de Mlle de Vinteuil' (1:113) ['little patches of a creamier colour, beneath which I imagined that this fragrance must lie concealed, as the taste of an almond cake lay beneath the burned parts, or of Mlle de Vinteuil's cheeks beneath their freckles' (1:123)]. All these associations seem to withdraw the hawthorn from the world of nature and to confine it to the world of culture. However, Marcel soon realizes that the 'intention de festivité dans les fleurs' ['festal scheme of decoration'] was not a human artifact but rather an expression of nature.

Mais, sans oser les regarder qu'à la dérobée, je sentais que ces apprêts pompeux étaient vivants et que c'était la nature elle-même qui, en creusant ces découpures dans les feuilles, en ajoutant l'ornement suprême de ces blancs boutons, avait rendu cette décoration digne de ce qui était à la fois une réjouissance populaire et une solemnité mystique. (1:112)

Though I dared not look at it save through my fingers, I could sense that this formal scheme was composed of living things, and that it was Nature herself who, by trimming the shape of the foliage, and by adding the crowning ornament of those snowy buds, had made the decorations worthy of what was at once a public rejoicing and a solemn mystery. (1:121)

It is significant that it is not vision which guides Marcel's revelation, but some kind of interior vision, 'à la dérobée,' a vision that undresses, removes the ornamentation, and makes him understand that it is part of nature's polymorphism. What thus started as a movement from nature to culture is brought back to nature.

Malgré la silencieuse immobilité des aubépines, cette intermit-
tente odeur était comme le murmure de leur vie intense dont
l'autel vibrait ainsi qu'une haie agreste visitée par de vivantes
antennes, auxquelles on pensait en voyant certaines étamines
presque rousses qui semblaient avoir gardé la virulence prin-
tanière, le pouvoir irritant, d'insectes aujourd'hui métamor-
phosés en fleurs. (1:113–14)

Despite the motionless silence of the hawthorns, these gusts of
fragrance came to me like the murmuring of an intense organic
life, with which the whole altar was quivering like a hedgerow
explored by living antennae, of which I was reminded by seeing
some stamens, almost red in colour, which seemed to have kept
the springtime virulence, the irritant power of stinging insects
now transmuted into flowers. (1:123)

This is typical of Marcel's description of flowers: they are
very rarely solitary cut flowers, always a cluster, and always
associated with insects either explicitly as here or implicitly: the bushes are always 'vibrant,' 'bourdonnant.' Moreover, it seems to be this harmonious relationship in nature,
this openness of the flower to the other, that causes Marcel's
desire for the presence of a woman. Thus, if Marcel's com-
munions with nature appear as solitary pastimes, they always lead to some desire for the other, or more precisely to
some reconciliation of the various tendencies within the
individual, especially the feminine and the masculine –
which nature rarely separates.

Mais si ce désir qu'une femme apparût ajoutait pour moi
aux charmes de la nature quelque chose de plus exaltant, les
charmes de la nature, en retour, élargissaient ce que celui de la
femme aurait eu de trop restreint. (1:156)

But if, for me, this desire that a woman should appear added
something more exalting to the charms of nature, they in their
turn enlarged what I might have found too restrictive in the
charms of a woman. (1:171)

This desire for a woman to appear, to grow out of the earth, as it were, and as Marcel suggests, becomes interiorized in a passage in which Marcel himself becomes metamorphosed into a woman in a way comparable to the mimetism at work in plants, based on the hermaphroditic morphology of the flower.

Plus haut s'ouvraient leurs corolles ça et là avec une grâce insouciante, retenant si négligemment, comme un dernier et vaporeux atour, le bouquet d'étamines, fines comme des fils de la Vierge, qui les embrumait tout entières, qu'en suivant, qu'en essayant de mimer au fond de moi le geste de leur efflorescence, je l'imaginais comme si ç'avait été le mouvement de tête étourdi et rapide, au regard coquet, aux pupilles diminuées, d'une blanche jeune fille, distraite et vive. (1:112)

Higher up on the altar, a flower had opened here and there with a careless grace, holding so unconcernedly, like a final, almost vaporous adornment, its bunch of stamens, slender as gossamer and entirely veiling each corolla, that in following, in trying to mimic to myself the action of their efflorescence, I imagined it as a swift and thoughtless movement of the head, with a provocative glance from her contracted pupils, by a young girl in white, insouciant and vivacious. (1:121)

In this dreamlike scene, an external 'landscape' is transplanted into the interior – a movement that often leads to understanding in Marcel. Out of the opening of the corolla (a female *topos*) emerge the stamens (a male *topos*). Similarly, but in an inverted way, Marcel's miming unfolds inside him a young woman. The 'pupilles diminuées,' the constricted pupils of the woman in this interior scene remind us of Marcel's description of Albertine asleep, where once again woman, sleep, dream, and flowers are associated:

Elle avait l'air d'une longue tige en fleurs qu'on avait disposée là; et c'était ainsi en effet: le pouvoir de rêver que je n'avais qu'en son absence, je le retrouvais à ces instants auprès d'elle, comme si en dormant elle était devenue une plante. (3:69–70)

She reminded me of a long blossoming stem that had been laid
there and so in a sense she was: the faculty of dreaming which I
possessed only in her absence, I recovered at such moments in
her presence, as though by falling asleep she had become a
plant. (3:64)

Albertine's lack of consciousness – marked by her lack of
vision – allows Marcel to communicate with her at the level
of the unconscious. If Marcel mentions that the kind of love
he then felt for Albertine 'était un amour pur, aussi imma-
tériel, aussi mystérieux que si j'avais été devant ces créa-
tures inanimées que sont les beautés de la nature' (3:70)
['was a love as pure, as immaterial, as mysterious, as if I had
been in the presence of those inanimate creatures which are
the beauties of nature' (3:64)], it is because, as in the presence of natural beauty, his desire is not one of possession,
but one of fusion or communion.

It would be wrong therefore to generalize about Proust's
association of flowers with women. Rather than being associated with one particular and singular sex, flowers subvert
the traditional opposition of the sexes and take Marcel back
to a hermaphroditic origin. One might even suggest that
Marcel's fascination with Albertine, his singling her out of
the bouquet of the 'jeunes filles en fleur' is linked to her bi-
sexuality. In the passage of the encounter between Charlus
and Jupien, the discussion of the natural laws presiding
over the fecundation of the orchid by the bee serves as a
pretext for such a reinterpretation of the sexual roles.

The inspiration for this analogy is Darwin's *The Various*
Contrivances by which Orchids Are Fertilized by Insects, to
which Proust refers. Darwin himself compares the artifices
imagined by orchids to seduce insects to the contrivances
of man's imagination to the advantage of nature:

The more I study nature, the more I become impressed with
ever-increasing force, that the contrivances and even beautiful
adaptations slowly acquired through each part occasionally

varying in a slight degree but in many ways with the preserva-
tion of these variations which were beneficial to the organism
under complex and ever varying conditions of life, transcend
in an incomparable manner the contrivances and adaptations
which the most fertile imagination of man could invent.[11]

Proust's comparison, on the other hand, leads him to re-
define 'ce qu'on appelle fort mal l'homosexualité' (2:607)
['what one calls wrongly homosexuality' (2:630)] as well as
aesthetic production and reception. What the encounter
between Charlus and Jupien, between the orchid and the
bee, and Marcel's encounter with 'the outside world' have in
common, at least as Marcel sees it at first, is their reliance
on chance. However, as Marcel realizes gradually, it is not
the kind of chance that is left entirely to chance, but rather,
as always in the world of nature – and of artistic production – an alliance of rule and chance.

What strikes Marcel at first is the fortuitousness of the
whole scene. He finds the fortuitous visit of the insect
carrying the adequate kind of pollen improbable. It is by
chance that he witnesses the encounter between Charlus
and Jupien. And, it is by chance that Charlus is at the duch-
ess's at that hour, and that Jupien has not yet left for work
after lunch. Nevertheless, as Marcel understands, the fertilization of the orchid, the encounter of the 'homosexuals'
and his 'revelation' are not left entirely to chance, rather
they depend on a fragile balance between external chance
and internal receptiveness. In these three realms there are
'dangers,' 'risks,' 'obstacles' that cannot be overcome by
chance alone: contrivances are needed.

It is striking that, at the beginning of the chapter, Marcel
is in the same situation as the female orchid: he is waiting
for the visit of the insect. However, as the scene develops,
the reader realizes that his waiting is no more passive than
that of the orchid which he describes:

Je résolus de ne plus me déranger de peur de manquer, si le
miracle devait se produire, l'arrivée presque impossible à es-

*pérer (à travers tant d'obstacles, de distance, de risques con-
traires, de dangers) de l'insecte envoyé de si loin en ambas-
sadeur à la vierge qui depuis longtemps prolongeait son attente. Je savais que cette attente n'était pas plus passive chez la
fleur mâle, dont les étamines s'étaient spontanément tournées
pour que l'insecte pût plus facilement la recevoir; de même la
fleur-femme qui était ici, si l'insecte venait, arquerait coquette-
ment ses 'styles,' et pour être mieux pénétrée par lui ferait im-
perceptiblement, comme une jouvencelle hypocrite mais ar-
dente, la moitié du chemin. (2:602–3)*

*I decided not to let myself be disturbed again for fear of miss-
ing, should the miracle be fated to occur, the arrival, almost
beyond the possibility of hope (across so many obstacles of
distance, of adverse risks, of dangers), of the insect sent from
so far away as ambassador to the virgin who had been waiting
for so long. I knew that this expectancy was no more passive
than in the male flower, whose stamens had spontaneously
curved so that the insect might more easily receive their offer-
ing; similarly the female flower that stood there would co-
quettishly arch her 'styles' if the insect came, and, to be more
effectively penetrated by him, would imperceptibly advance,
like a hypocritical but ardent damsel, to meet him half-way.*
(2:624)

If Marcel knows intellectually the contrivances at work in
the natural world, he has not yet grasped their role in the
'miracle,' which he attributes to fortuitousness, nor their
purpose. Interestingly, it is through his understanding of
the mixture of conscious and unconscious elements, a mixture of chance and predetermination presiding over the recognition of Charlus and Jupien that Marcel – who as a result
has missed the visit of the actual bee to the orchid – can be
certain that the natural miracle has happened. It is also only
when Marcel realizes the contrivances and metamorphoses
involved in the encounter between Charlus and Jupien that
the scene gains beauty and meaning for him. The passage

describing Marcel's 'révélation' – his fertilization – is long but worth quoting here, as it shows the gradual understanding of the production of beauty through an encounter between heterogeneous elements.

J'allais me déranger de nouveau pour qu'il ne pût m'apercevoir; je n'en eus ni le temps, ni le besoin. Que vis-je! Face à face, dans cette cour où ils ne s'étaient certainement jamais rencontrés (M. de Charlus ne venant à l'hôtel Guermantes que dans l'après-midi, aux heures où Jupien était à son bureau), le baron ayant soudain largement ouvert ses yeux mis-clos, regardait avec une attention extraordinaire l'ancien giletier sur le seuil de sa boutique, cependant que celui-ci, cloué subitement sur place devant M. de Charlus, enraciné comme une plante, contemplait d'un air émerveillé l'embonpoint du baron vieillissant. Mais, chose plus étonnante encore, l'attitude de M. de Charlus, ayant changé, celle de Jupien se mit aussitôt, comme selon les lois d'un art secret, en harmonie avec elle. Le baron, qui cherchait maintenant à dissimuler l'impression qu'il avait ressentie, mais qui, malgré son indifférence affectée, semblait ne s'éloigner qu'à regret, allait, venait, regardait dans le vague de la façon qu'il pensait mettre le plus en valeur la beauté de ses prunelles, prenait un air fat, négligent, ridicule. Or Jupien, perdant aussitôt l'air humble et bon que je lui avais toujours connu, avait – en symétrie parfaite avec le baron – redressé la tête, donnait à sa taille un port avantageux, posait avec une impertinence grotesque son poing sur la hanche, faisait saillir son derrière, prenait des poses avec la coquetterie qu'aurait pu avoir l'orchidée pour le bourdon providentiellement survenu. Je ne savais pas qu'il pût avoir l'air si antiphatique. Mais j'ignorais aussi qu'il fût capable de tenir à l'improviste sa partie dans cette sorte de scène des deux muets, qui (bien qu'il se trouvât pour la première fois en présence de M. de Charlus) semblait avoir été longuement répétée; – on n'arrive spontanément à cette perfection que quand on rencontre à l'étranger un compatriote, avec lequel alors l'entente se fait d'elle-même, le truchement étant identique, et sans qu'on se

soit pourtant jamais vu, la scène préétablie. Cette scène n'était,
du reste, pas positivement comique, elle était empreinte d'une
étrangeté, ou, si l'on veut d'un naturel, dont la beauté allait
croissant. (2:604–5)

I was about to change my position again, so that he should not
catch sight of me; I had neither the time nor the need to do so.
For what did I see! Face to face, in that courtyard where they
had certainly never met before (M. de Charlus coming to the
Hôtel de Guermantes only in the afternoon, during the time
when Jupien was at his office), the Baron, having suddenly
opened wide his half-shut eye, was gazing with extraordinary
attentiveness at the ex-tailor poised on the threshold of his
shop, while the latter, rooted suddenly to the spot in front of
M. de Charlus, implanted there like a tree, contemplated with
a look of wonderment the plump form of the aging Baron. But,
more astounding still, M. de Charlus's pose having altered,
Jupien's, as though in obedience to the laws of an occult art, at
once brought itself into harmony with it. The Baron, who now
sought to disguise the impression that had been made on him,
and yet, in spite of his affectation of indifference, seemed un-
able to move away without regret, came and went, looked
vaguely into the distance, in the way which he felt would most
enhance the beauty of his eyes, assumed a smug, nonchalant,
fatuous air. Meanwhile Jupien, shedding at once the humble,
kindly expression which I had always associated with him,
had – in perfect symmetry with the Baron – thrown back his
head, given a becoming tilt to his body, placed his hand with
grotesque effrontery on his hip, stuck out his behind, struck
poses with the coquetry that the orchid might have adopted on
the providential arrival of the bee. I had not supposed that he
could appear so repellent. But I was equally unaware that he
was capable of improvising his part in this sort of dumb show
which (although he found himself for the first time in the presence of M. de Charlus) seemed to have been long and carefully
rehearsed; one does not arrive spontaneously at that pitch of
perfection except when one meets in a foreign country a com-

patriot with whom an understanding then develops of itself,
the means of communication being the same and, even though
one has never seen the other before, the scene already set. The
scene was not, however, positively comic, it was stamped with
a strangeness, or if you like, a naturalness, the beauty of which
steadily increased. (2:626–27)

The beauty, even the perfection, of the scene, which Marcel first finds ridiculous, resides in the role of some unconscious memory, some secret and invisible law – which allows the bee to 'recognize' the flower, which allows the 'homosexuals' to recognize each other as 'of the same species' and perfectly adapted to one another – it is the same secret law which, as Marcel understands later, directs the perfect sentence.

In the natural world, some insects, such as the bee, precisely, are guided by experience & memory. In *The Effects of Cross- and Self-Fertilization,* Darwin wonders, like Proust, about the miracle of 'recognition': 'But how do they discover at first that the above varieties with different colored flowers belong to the same species? Improbable as it may seem, they seem, at least sometimes, to recognize plants even from a distance by their general aspect, in the same manner as we should do.'[12] It is the same mixture of imprudence, chance, and unconscious memory that allows Marcel to derive meaning & beauty from the scene. In the same way that the scene between the two homosexuals seems 'longuement répétée,' Marcel's recognition depends on memory. It is again through an analogy that this scene makes sense for Marcel:

Si je ne le fus pas [vu], je pense que je le dois plus au hasard
qu'à ma sagesse. Et au fait que j'aie pris un parti si imprudent,
quand le cheminement dans la cave était si sûr, je vois trois
raisons possibles, à supposer qu'il y en ait une. Mon impa-
tience d'abord. Puis peut-être un obscur ressouvenir de la scène
de Montjouvain, caché devant la fenêtre de Mlle Vinteuil. De

fait, les choses de ce genre auxquelles j'assistai eurent toujours, dans la mise en scène, le caractère le plus imprudent et le moins vraisemblable, comme si de telles révélations ne devaient être la récompense que d'un acte plein de risques, quoique en partie clandestin. (2:607–8)

If I was not [seen], I owe it more, I am sure, to chance than to my own sagacity. And for the fact that I took so imprudent a course, when the way through the cellar was so safe, I can see three possible reasons, assuming that I had any reason at all. First of all, my impatience. Secondly, perhaps, a dim memory of the scene at Montjouvain, when I crouched concealed outside Mlle Vinteuil's window. Certainly, the affairs of this sort of which I have been a spectator have always been, as far as their setting is concerned, of the most imprudent and least probable character, as if such revelations were to be the reward of an action full of risk, though in part clandestine. (2:630)

What then is this reward (*récompense*), this revelation that Marcel is talking about here? And what is the reason – if there is any, as he says – for his interest in this scene? In the natural world, the reward to the plant, and its unconscious purpose for seducing the insect, is fertilization and perpetuation of the species; for the insect, the reward is the nectar that the flower provides as a nourishment in return for the pollinating service; for the homosexuals, the reward is sexual pleasure and liberation from exclusion. As for Marcel's reward, it is similar at once to the insect's & to the flower's. Like the insect, who falls upon the invisible nectar at the bottom of the corolla, Marcel falls upon some invisible truth: 'Ce que je viens de dire d'ailleurs ici est ce que je ne devais comprendre que quelques minutes plus tard, tant adhèrent à la réalité ces propriétés d'être invisibles, jusqu'à ce qu'une circonstance l'ait depouillée d'elles' (2:607) ['All that I have just said, however, I was not to understand until several minutes had elapsed, to such an extent is reality encumbered by those properties of invisibility until a chance occurrence has divested it of them'] (2:629). For Proust, the revelation is an unveiling of truth, of what Heidegger calls *aletheia*, which eventually becomes equated with the unfolding of a metaphor:

En M. de Charlus un autre être avait beau s'accoupler, qui le différenciait des autres hommes, comme dans le centaure le cheval, cet être avait beau faire corps avec le baron, je ne l'avais jamais aperçu. Maintenant l'abstrait s'était matérialisé, l'être enfin compris avait aussitôt perdu son pouvoir de rester invisible, et la transmutation de M. de Charlus en une personne nouvelle était si complète que non seulement les contrastes de son visage, de sa voix, mais rétrospectivement les hauts et les bas eux-mêmes de ses relations avec moi, tout ce qui avait paru jusque-là incohérent à mon esprit, devenait intelligible, se montrait évident, comme une phrase, n'offrant aucun sens tant qu'elle reste décomposée en lettres disposées au hasard, exprime, si les caractères se trouvent replacés dans l'ordre qu'il faut, une pensée que l'on ne pourra plus oublier. (2:614)

Although in the person of M. de Charlus another creature was coupled, as the horse in the centaur, which made him different from other men, although this creature was one with the Baron, I had never perceived it. Now the abstraction had become materialized, the creature at last discerned had lost its power of remaining invisible, and the transformation of M. de Charlus into a new person was so complete that not only the contrasts of his face and of his voice, but, in retrospect, the very ups and downs of his relations with myself, everything that hitherto had seemed to my mind incoherent, became intelligible, appeared self-evident, just as a sentence which presents no meaning so long as it remains broken up in letters arranged at random expresses, if the letters be rearranged in the proper order, a thought which one can never afterwards forget. (2:637)

Here, as we had surmised, all is a question of mode of signification, a question of style as an ordering of letters that unveils the truth, & ensures its survival. Understanding the nature – and difference – of M. de Charlus, like reading and writing, goes beyond mere sight, which has a tendency to remain on the surface and separate what is actually fused. From the preparation of the style of the flower for the reception of the pollen, and thus for the encounter, Marcel learns about the necessary receptivity of the mind to the external reality, and about the role of literary style in signification. From the style of the flower, which Proust placed within quotation marks in the passage I previously quoted, to literary style, the journey is short, and ends in metaphor. Truth is indeed attained through the transformation of a concept, an abstraction into a living embodiment. Truth reveals itself only through a metaphor, a metamorphosis. Metaphor and metamorphosis are thus not disguises; on the contrary, they are what allows truth to take place, what unveils the invisible truth that was always there but did not reveal itself. The metamorphoses in this passage, as in the world of nature, do not change people and things into what they are not; on the contrary, they reveal the hidden presence of the other in the self. The metamorphoses of Charlus into a woman shows the invisible 'woman' within Charlus, whereas his transmutation into a 'bourdon' (a male bee) reveals his virility – till finally maleness & femaleness, which appear as separated in the world of mere vision, are seen to belong to one single and originary hermaphroditic being. One must note that the metamorphoses are unstable so that one cannot say that Jupien is the orchid and Charlus the *bourdon*, or vice versa. At first, the seductive attitude of the Baron leads Marcel to compare him to an orchid; later his whistling leads to his transmutation into a *bourdon*. Here, as in the natural world, the harmony is so complete that it becomes impossible to tell one from the other.

This is why the choice of the fertilization of the orchid by the bee is such a natural choice, since a similar subversion of contraries, a similar transgression of cultural categories, is at work. If the transformation of Jupien/Charlus into the fragile, feminine, classy orchid appears ludicrous and even comical, the natural metamorphoses of the orchid itself are just as surprising. Its name alone introduces its openness to difference. Its name is feminine in French, and because of its fragility, beauty, and methods of seduction, it is traditionally ascribed 'feminine' qualities. However, its name derives from the Greek *orchis* which means testicles, probably because of the testicular shape of its roots. As a result, according to the doctrine of signatures, which saw in the shape of plants a sign of their medicinal functions, orchids were sought as a remedy against waning virility, and more generally known for their aphrodisiac qualities – an effect they had on the insects who pollinated them. According to plant lore, orchids grew out of bulls' semen that escaped during copulation and was spilled on the ground. From this alone we can deduce the kind of sexual ambiguity that orchids' strange comportment reinforces. Their mimetic contrivances fascinated Darwin: orchids mime the female insect of the male species by which they 'want' to be pollinated. In some cases, the miming is so perfectly contrived that the male insects prefer the flowers to their female counterparts, sometimes even reach the desired orgasm. Under the heading 'L'ambiguité sexuelle des orchidées,' Jean-Marie Pelt concludes,

Mâles par leur signature testiculaire, femelles par leurs attitudes séductrices, voici les orchidées singulièrement ambigües. En fait le sexe dépend ici de l'observateur: il est femelle pour l'insecte, mais mâle pour l'homme. Symbole même de la séduction, avec tout ce qu'elle a d'équivoque, l'orchidée est une sorte de Janus à deux visages, femme fatale et Don Juan. Pour tout dire, un être trouble et profondément troublant.

Male by their testicular signature, female by their seduction, orchids are particularly ambiguous. In fact, their sex depends

on the observer: it is female for the insect, but male for man. As a symbol of seduction itself and of all that is equivocal about it, the orchid is a kind of two-faced Janus: femme fatale *and Don Juan. In other words, a being at the same time indistinct and disturbing.*[13]

This dual nature fascinated Darwin, especially since orchids are on the one hand so extravagantly adapted to cross-fertilization, even though they are hermaphroditic & thus could be self-fertilized. Out of this paradox, Darwin deduces the laws of evolution and the moral lesson that 'nature abhors perpetual self-fertilization.' What he is forced to realize is that what nature abhors above all is sterility, and the death of the species. Similarly, for Proust, the highest natural and social laws are those that allow difference, prevent solitude, exclusion, and the solipsism of the mind – the threat to 'homosexuals,' artists, and rare salon orchids.

Les lois du monde végétal sont gouvernées elles-mêmes par des lois de plus en plus hautes. Si la visite d'un insecte, c'est-à-dire l'apport de la semence d'une autre fleur, est habituellement nécessaire pour féconder une fleur, c'est que l'autofécondation, la fécondation de la fleur par elle-même, comme les mariages répétés dans une même famille, amènerait la dégénérescence et la stérilité, tandis que le croisement opéré par les insectes donne aux générations suivantes de la même espèce une vigueur inconnue de leurs ainées. Cependant cet essor peut être excessif, l'espèce se développer démesurément; alors, comme une antitoxine défend contre la maladie, comme le corps thyroïde règle notre embonpoint, comme la défaite vient punir l'orgueil, la fatigue le plaisir, et comme le sommeil repose à son tour de la fatigue, ainsi un acte exceptionnel d'autofécondation vient à point nommé donner son tour de vis, son coup de frein, fait rentrer dans la norme la fleur qui en était exagérément sortie. (2:603)

The laws of the vegetable kingdom are themselves governed by increasingly higher laws. If the visit of an insect, that is to say

the transportation of the seed from another flower, is generally
necessary for the fertilization of a flower, that is because self-
fertilization, the insemination of a flower by itself, would lead,
like a succession of intermarriages in the same family, to de-
generacy and sterility, whereas the crossing effected by insects
gives to the subsequent generations of the same species a vig-
our unknown to their forebears. This invigoration may, how-
ever, prove excessive, & the species develop out of all pro-
portion; then, as an anti-toxin protects us against disease, as
the thyroid gland regulates our adiposity, as defeat comes to
punish pride, as fatigue follows indulgence, and as sleep in
turn brings rest from fatigue, so an exceptional act of self-
fertilization comes at the crucial moment to apply its turn of
the screw, its pull on the curb, brings back within the norm the
flower that has exaggeratedly overstepped it. (2:624–25)

Thus, in 'Le Temps retrouvé,' Marcel notes the necessity
of the erotic descent in the production of the work of art:
'Aussi combien s'en tiennent là qui n'extraient rien de leur
impression, vieillissent inutiles et insatisfaits, comme des
célibataires de l'Art! Ils ont les chagrins qu'ont les vierges
et les paresseux, et que la fécondité ou le travail guérirait'
(3:892) ['And how many art-lovers stop there, without extracting anything from their impression, so that they grow
old useless and unsatisfied, like life-long bachelors! They
suffer, but their sufferings, like the sufferings of virgins and
lazy people, are of a kind that fecundity or work would
cure' (3:927)]. The virginity of the mind, as well as the self-
fertilization of the flower is a sin. The fortuitous, but necessary, cross-fertilization of the flower points the way to the
cross-fertilization of the mind, so that the work of art can
occur. Or, using Proustian critical terms, this is the same as
realizing the inadequacy of voluntary memory in the elaboration of the work of art. This explains why the birth, and
ensured truth, of the work of art in Proust is always expressed, on the one hand, as a fortuitous exfoliation, or
floral birth, and on the other, as an excavation of truth from

the depth of the unconscious. The work of art is indeed always in Proust the excavation of the past self scattered in the world through the act of living and seeing, just as it is also always the recollection of the 'petit sillon que la vue d'une aubépine ou d'une église a creusé en nous' (3:891) ['the little furrow which the sight of a hawthorn bush or of a church has traced in us' (3:927)]. As such the work of art always tells the story of the cross-fertilization of the mind by the outside world and of the outside world by the mind. Just as the flower cannot will fertilization or blossoming, Marcel cannot will recollection. As one sees in the passage of the madeleine, the buried remnants of the past will only blossom out through a descent into the silent forces of the unconscious. Moreover, this blossoming out entails a metamorphosis. This retrieval of the buried remnants of the past and of the self can only happen, as in the case of Orpheus attempting to retrieve Eurydice, through the negation of individual desire and conscious will. This recollection of the truth of the self is an *aletheia,* not simply in the sense of an unveiling, but as a retrieval from darkness. In this way, truth, *aletheia,* can only emerge from Lethe, the river of forgetfulness.

It is this mythic descent that Proust describes in an introduction to the experience of the madeleine:

Je trouve très raisonnable la croyance celtique que les âmes de ceux que nous avons perdus sont captives dans quelque être inférieur, dans une bête, un végétal, une chose inanimée, perdues en effet pour nous jusqu'au jour, qui pour beaucoup ne vient jamais, où nous nous trouvons passer près de l'arbre, entrer en possession de l'objet qui est leur prison. Alors elles tressaillent, nous appellent, et sitôt que nous les avons reconnues, l'enchantement est brisé. Délivrées par nous, elles ont vaincu la mort et reviennent vivre avec nous. (1:44)

I feel there is much to be said for the Celtic belief that the souls of those whom we have lost are held captive in some inferior being, in an animal, in a plant, in some inanimate object, and thus effectively lost to us until the day (which to many never comes) when we happen to pass by the tree or to obtain posses-sion of the object which forms their prison. Then they start to tremble, they call us by our name, and as soon as we have recognized their voice the spell is broken. Delivered by us, they have overcome death and return to share our life. (1:47)

The famous madeleine passage describes such a liberation of the captive soul of Marcel: this liberation is described in terms of an exfoliation. The work of art, like the flower, moves from the world of darkness where it takes its roots to the world of light to which it aspires. If the work of art, as Marcel notes, is always present within the writer, as the shapes of butterflies, flowers, and birds are always already present in the pressed pieces of paper in the Japanese game, it takes the mediation of the tea and the madeleine for the past to be reborn, and the presence of water for the Japanese butterflies to take flight.

I f in Proust, the flower presents a relationship between the underworld & the world of light, it remains, how-ever, mainly associated with vision & contemplation. This contemplation is however not the kind of scientific observation that Foucault describes, the kind of observa-tion that separates subject and object. On the contrary, it is the kind of inner vision that establishes a reciprocal rela-tionship between subject and object, between inner and outer, out of which understanding, meaning, and eventu-ally art can emerge. It is the kind of contemplation that does not remain on the surface of things, but brings out the invisible truth hidden underneath. Georges Poulet empha-sizes this intimacy between Marcel and the objects of per-ception: 'It all comes finally to the question: how can an exterior object be transmuted into this interior and imma-terial thing, as intimate to us as ourselves, in which the mind freely plunges, moves, takes delight and life?'[14] In

Rilke, on the other hand, the flower becomes associated with the ear, and both flower and ear form and cross the thresholds between inside and outside, above and underneath. In the *Sonette an Orpheus,* the descent of Orpheus into the Underworld to retrieve his lost Eurydice becomes Rilke's own descent into his unconscious out of which the work of art arises.[15]

Remembering that Rilke was supposed to go into psychoanalysis with Freud, but refused, we might say that he chose instead to write his own descent into the unconscious, a venture that Freud himself often described in archaeological terms. There seems to be a link between digging the fragmented remnants of the past, even attempting to piece them together, going through psychoanalysis, and writing as a way of discovering one's own unconscious, going back to the mythical past. This is the way Rilke presents his motivation in a letter to Lou Andreas-Salomé:

Ich weiß jetzt, daß die Analyse für mich nur Sinn hätte, wenn der merkwürdige Hintergedanke, nicht mehr zu schreiben, den ich mir während der Beendigung des Malte *öfters als eine Art Erleichterung vor die Nase hängte, mir wirklich ernst wäre. Dann dürfte man sich die Teufel austreiben lassen, da sie ja im Bürgerlichen wirklich nur störend und peinlich sind, und gehen die Engel möglicherweise mit aus, so müßte man auch das als Vereinfachung auffassen und nicht sagen, daß sie ja in jenem neuen nächsten Beruf (welchem?) sicher nicht in Verwendung kämen.*

I know now that psychoanalysis would make sense for me only if I were really serious about the strange possibility of no longer writing, which during the completion of Malte *I often dangled in front of my nose as a kind of relief. Then one might let one's devils be exorcised, since in daily life, they are truly just disturbing and painful. And if it happened that the angels left too, one would have to understand this as a further simplification and tell oneself that in the new profession (which?) there would certainly be no use for them.*[16]

Moreover, if we believe Rilke that *Sonette an Orpheus* represents 'vielleicht das geheimste, mir selber, in ihr Aufkommen und sich-mir-Auftragen, rätselhafte Diktat, daß ich je ausgehalten und geleistet habe' ['the most mysterious, most enigmatic dictation that arose & imposed itself on me'], we already understand part of their cosmology: a voice from below reaches the ear of the poet; Eurydice, transformed into Persephone, crosses the threshold of the earth as a flower arises in the mind.[17]

It might be worth noting that, at the time he was writing *Sonette,* Rilke was reading books on natural science & biology. His reading of Goethe's 'Metamorphose der Pflanzen' influenced his interpretation of the Orpheus myth just as his reading of Grimm's dictionary influenced his concern with language. From Goethe, he learned a theory of the organic metamorphosis of the plant from the *Urpflanz;* from Jakob Grimm he learned a theory of the polymorphic growth of language(s) from the *Ursprache.* Hence in Rilke's poems an association between the linguistic and the organic, and the link between the flower and the ear. Goethe himself had established the link between language and plants, not only through his interest in both domains, but in a work significantly titled 'Urworte: Orphish.' Goethe's 'Metamorphose der Pflanzen' is based on the idea of perpetual becoming. Thus Goethe writes, 'What has just been formed is instantly transformed' and 'Metamorphosis is the key to the whole alphabet of nature.'[18] In *The Orphic Voice,* Elizabeth Sewell sees a relationship between Goethe's botanical essays and Rilke's *Sonette:* 'What Rilke suggests in and through Orpheus is a morphogenesis of the organic life of the mind, an Orphic epistemology whose dynamic is that of metamorphoses in a continuum . . . his two orphic ancestors are Ovid and Goethe.'[19]

As the poem 'Wendung' (The Turning Point) indicates, vision is limited to space, whereas the ear can hear the echoes of the past. The eye is associated with the realm of consciousness and supervision, with the Apollonian light of vision. It is therefore too abstract and condescending to represent and comprehend the unconscious birth of the work of art. In 'Wendung,' Rilke concludes,

> Denn des Anschauns, siehe, ist eine Grenze.
> Und die geschautere Welt
> will in der Liebe gedeihn.

> Werk des Gesichts ist getan,
> tue nun Herz-Werk
> an den Bildern in dir, jenen gefangenen, denn du
> überwältigtest sie: aber nun kennst du sie nicht.
> Siehe, innerer Mann, dein inneres Mädchen,
> dieses errungene aus
> tausend Naturen, dieses
> erst nur errungene, nie
> noch geliebte Geschöpf. (sw 2:82–84)

> For there is a boundary to looking.
> And the world that is looked at so deeply
> wants to flourish in love.

> Work of the eye is done, now
> go and do heart-work
> on all the images imprisoned within you; for you
> overpowered them: but even now you don't know them.
> Learn, inner man, to look on your inner woman,
> the one attained from a thousand
> natures, the merely attained but
> not yet beloved form. (Mitchell, Selected Poetry, 133)

As this poem shows, not only is vision limited as a means of apprehending the world, but it sets limits, boundaries between things. Vision encloses things, entraps them, separates and frames. As such it prevents real knowledge, which relies on proximity to things, and allows 'the world that is looked at to flourish in love' ['Und die geschautere Welt / will in der Liebe gedeihn']. The ear – like the flower – on the other hand, allows simultaneity to exist without imposing precedence. Physically, the ear is always ready and receptive – not only to outer but also to inner sounds. The ears are 'the eyes of darkness,' as Joyce had it. It is in a sense impossible to close one's ears, while it is quite possible to close one's eyes. With our eyes, we are a subject in a world of objects, with our ears, we are in the world, we belong to it, and cannot keep it out even if we wished to.

However, in this poem, the contrast to the eye is not yet as in *Sonette,* the ear, but the heart. The heart, as the site of love, represents the same proximity between inner and outer. Commenting on this poem in 'What Are Poets For?' Heidegger opposes the work of the eye, which he qualifies as 'the still covetous vision of things' to the work of the heart which makes possible the 'inward conversion to the open,' that is, 'the great whole of all that is unbounded.'[20] More important, for Rilke, the heart is the locus where man – the inner man – will discover 'the inner woman.' It is only when he is removed from the world of reasoned vision that man will be able to retrieve the feminine in him. For Rilke, plants, animals, and women, especially mothers, are 'in the world,' or in the open, actually belong to it, whereas men are separated from it. This is why, man, in Rilke, must learn from woman or find the woman within him, especially since for him, the creative activity is like 'giving birth.' One is here reminded of Proust's proximity to Albertine when, in her sleep, she makes him think of a flower, as well as of Proust's transformation into a woman when he is looking at the hawthorns. In both Proust and Rilke, the journey to the underworld is rewarded by the discovery of an unconscious androgyny, and the realization of the feminine origin of the work of art.

Rilke's *Sonette an Orpheus* presents the turning inward, the turning away from the world of vision that 'Wendung' announces. The sonnets are in fact a hymn, a celebration of Orpheus's musical creative power – which is also the power of metamorphosis. According to the myth – which Rilke alters and reinterprets – Orpheus failed to retrieve Eurydice because, after charming Pluto and Persephone into letting Eurydice follow him out of Hades, he looked back. Orpheus thus loses Eurydice because he looks back, doubts, seeks to ascertain the possession of what his music had already retrieved. Already in the myth, therefore, the eye casts doubts on the power of the ear.

This is why the *Sonette* could not be written from the point of view of Orpheus, and why also Orpheus is not for Rilke a symbol for the poet. The sonnets are addressed to Orpheus, as to a younger poet who has the power of music but has not yet learned to trust it, as Rilke has. Indeed, in his letter explaining how *Sonette an Orpheus* was written down from a 'dictation,' Rilke writes: 'Der ganze erste Teil ist, in einem einzigen atemlosen *Gehorchen,* zwischen dem 2 und dem 5 Februar 1922 niedergeschrieben, *ohne das ein Wort im Zweifel oder zu ändern war*' ['The whole first part was written down in a single breathless *obedience,* between the 2nd and the 5th of February 1922, *without one word being in doubt or having to be changed*'].[21] Rilke did not attempt to control the Eurydice alive in his unconscious: he let her speak within him.

In Rilke's version of the myth, Orpheus cannot – and should not – will to retrieve Eurydice, since that would entail her loss. Eurydice is here not simply the female figure who, as she was gathering flowers, was bitten by a serpent and swallowed up by the earth, she also comes to resemble Persephone, whose fate was similar. Eurydice takes roots in the Underworld at the moment when Orpheus looks back. As such, she recalls Persephone who is associated with the natural cycle of death and rebirth which overpowers individual will and desire.

When, in Sonnet 2.13, Rilke writes, 'Sei immer tot in Eurydike' [Be forever dead in Eurydice], one realizes that death – the death of Eurydice – is not supposed to be seen as the opposite or negation of life, but rather as the necessary concealment out of which its rising can take place. As Heidegger suggests, 'Death and the realm of the dead belong to the whole of beings as its other side'; it is 'the unillumined side of life.'[22] This is the law of nature: it is out of the concealment of the seed that the flower and the fruit will grow; it is out of a similar 'gestation' in the poet's unconscious that the poem can come to light. In the *Letters to a Young Poet,* Rilke illustrates the birth of the poem as the organic growth of a seed.

Alles ist austragen und dann gebären. Jeden Eindruck und jeden Keim eines Gefühls ganz in sich, im Dunkel, im Unsagbaren, Unbewußten, dem eigenen Verstande Unereichbaren sich vollenden lassen und mit tiefer Demut und Geduld die Stunde der Niederkunft einer neuen Klarheit abwarten: das allein heißt künstlerisch leben: im Verstehen wie im Schaffen.

Everything is gestation and then birthing. To let each impression and each embryo of a feeling come to completion, entirely in itself, in the dark, in the unsayable, the unconscious, beyond the reach of one's own understanding, and with deep humility and patience wait for the hour when a new clarity is born: this alone is what it means to live as an artist: in understanding as in creating.[23]

The process described here reminds us of the transformation of an outer impression within the inner mind, till it is brought forth in a metaphor in Proust's *A la recherche*. In both cases, a natural process is at work in which the bringing forth of life and truth depends on a necessary concealment.

In his reading of a fragment from Heraclitus, 'physis kruptesthai philei' (nature likes hiding), Heidegger comments on the necessary concealment involved in natural bringing forth. '*Kruptesthai* is, as self-concealing, not a mere self-closing, but a sheltering in which the essential possibility of rising is preserved – to which rising as such belongs. . . . Self-revealing never dispenses with concealing, but actually needs it in order to occur in the way it occurs as dis-closing.'[24] This passage helps us understand why in Rilke's poetry, flowers – and women – are always associated with the production of the work of art as a 'bringing forth' out of concealment and a return of the past. In their closing, infolding, they point to the necessity of sheltering out of which unfolding can occur. Indeed, Eurydice, especially in her transformation into a flower, also represents the feminine and Protean unconscious with which man has to come to terms. Half woman, half flower, half alive, half dead, half visible, half invisible, Eurydice (not Orpheus) represents the ideal equivocation of the Rilkean poet, the figure of transition between virginity & motherhood, life & death, above and below. By allowing Eurydice this liminal freedom, Rilke gives his own poetics a mythic authority to reconcile – without annulling – the contraries with which his poetry abounds.

It is because of his association with the Underworld, because of his link with Eurydice – his unconscious – that Orpheus has the power of creation, the power of metamorphosing the invisible (concealed truth) into the visible (bringing forth of unveiled truth). In Sonnet 1.6, Rilke portrays Orpheus as belonging to both realms: the realm above ground and the Underworld. As such he is already a metaphor – the possibility of a communication, a passage from one realm to the other. This is what his gift of metamorphosis consists of – the passage from inner to outer, from above to underneath:

> Ist er ein Hiesiger? Nein aus beiden
> Reichen erwuchs seine weite Natur
> Kundiger boge die Zweige der Weiden
> Wer die Wurzeln der Weiden erfuhr. (sw 1:734)

> Is this where he belongs? No, his wide nature
> has grown from elements of both great realms,
> who digs among the willow's roots, that creature
> is best prepared to weave the willow's limbs.[25]

It is because he has experienced the concealment of the willow's roots in the Underworld that Orpheus can move its branches and give it life. His power of animating the inanimate is therefore based on a retrieval of the invisible animate and human power that nature always possessed – but concealed.

Orpheus is associated with the power of transformation in a twofold manner. On the one hand, through the seductive power of his song, he gives human form to animate and inanimate things. On the other, his dismemberment points to the transcendence of death by song as well as to the ubiquitous presence of song in the world. This power of transformation is, however, none other than a making visible – an unveiling – of a human shape that was already there at the start. Thus, in order to rescue Daphne from the laurel tree, one has to descend into the underworld of language and myth, to take language back to its origin in music – or, even further, in breath: 'Und die verwandelte Daphne / will, seit sie Lorbeern fühlt, daß du dich wandelst in Wind' (Sonnet 2.12, sw I:759) ['And Daphne, leaved transformation, / feeling herself a tree, wants you changed into a wind' (*Sonnets,* 39)]. We should remind ourselves that, in the myth, Daphne was changed into a laurel tree by her father, the river god Peneus, when she was pursued by Apollo, the light of the sun. The eye alone cannot retrieve or possess Daphne – it can only destroy her, as Apollo's rays alone would have. But the wind can. The poet can caress Daphne only by becoming music, breath, the wind: 'In Wahrheit singen, ist ein andrer Hauch. / Ein Hauch um nichts. Ein Wehn im Gott. Ein Wind' (Sonnet 1:3, sw I:732) ['True singing is a different breath, about / nothing. A gust inside the god. A wind' (*Sonnets,* 231)]. And Rilke's ideal is 'Atmen, du unsichbares Gedicht' (Sonnet 2:1, sw I:751) ['Breath, invisible poem'].

In order to capture this ephemeral passage of one thing into another, Rilke uses the power of music, which in the

poem 'An die Musik' he calls 'Du Sprache wo Sprachen /
enden,' 'O du der Gefühle / Wandlung . . . in hörbare Land-
schaft' (sw II:111) ['You language where all language / ends'
'O you the transformation of feelings . . . into audible landscape' (*Sonnets* 147)]. Like Orpheus's song, Rilke's poetry
has to become the 'invisible breath' that caresses the tree.
Indeed, the task of the poet is to eliminate that void between inner and outer, to impregnate the ear so that the tree
can be born. To be 'the ear of the earth' is to be poised precisely at this threshold between inner and outer, above and
underneath, at the point exactly where, in the spring, Persephone is allowed to cross the surface of the earth, at this
point where the text can flower, and the earth can speak
through us.

As in most myths of the Underworld, the descent is also
a descent into language, a going back to the roots of signification. Leaving the world of reason, light, and consciousness behind requires that we take advantage of the play of
the signifier & allow the unconscious to motivate signification. As Herbert Marcuse remarks in *Eros and Civilization,*
'Orpheus is associated with liberation, his work is song and
his language is play.'[26] In Rilke's Orpheus poems, as in *Alice
in Wonderland,* and other underground tales or myths, the
descent into the cavernous and fertile world of the ear takes
one to a world of puns, echoes, and resonances, which force
us to read not only with the eye, but also with the ear.

The first sonnet is a good example of this birth of art out
of the underground of the ear and of the reconciliation of
opposites:

> *Da stieg ein Baum. O reine Übersteigung!*
> *O Orpheus singt! O Hoher Baum im Ohr!*
> *Und alles schwieg. Doch selbst in der Verschweigung*
> *ging neuer Anfang, Wink und Wandlung vor.*
>
> *Tiere aus Stille drangen aus dem klaren*
> *gelösten Wald von Lager und Genist;*

und da ergab sich, daß sie nicht aus List
und nicht aus Angst in sich so leise waren,

sondern aus Hören. Brüllen, Schrei, Geröhr
schien klein in ihren Herzen. Und wo eben
kaum eine Hütte war, dies zu empfangen,

ein Unterschlupf aus dunkelstem Verlangen,
mit einem Zugang, dessen Pfosten beben, –
da schufst du ihnen Tempel im Gehör. (SW 1:731)

A tree ascended there. Oh pure transcendence!
Oh Orpheus sings! Oh tall tree in the ear!
And all things hushed. Yet even in that silence
a new beginning, beckoning, change appeared.

Creatures of stillness crowded from the bright
unbound forest, out of their lairs and nests;
and it was not from any dullness, not
from fear, that they were so quiet in themselves,

but from simply listening. Bellow, roar, shriek
seemed small inside their hearts. And where there had been
just a makeshift hut to receive the music,

a shelter nailed up out of their darkest longing,
with an entryway that shuddered in the wind –
you built a temple deep inside their hearing.
(Mitchell, *Selected Poetry*, 227)

This sonnet is presented as a hymn to Orpheus in which Rilke attempts to reenact for us the acoustic creation of Orpheus. For that to be possible, he must, like Orpheus, prepare our ear: like Orpheus, in the last line of the poem, he has to 'erect temples for us in our inner ear.' It is only in this silence and recollection that creation can happen. That silence, however, is not the absence of sound or of language, it is precisely the site of a 'new beginning, a beckoning, a metamorphosis.' The metamorphosis here is a turning of everything into its opposite, a reconciliation of things that appear separate in the upper world of light. Thus, the tree is not outside but inside our ear; what seems cavernous like the ear actually protrudes, like the tree; the hut becomes a temple.

If it is going to be successful, however, the poem has to repeat Orpheus's gesture and make us *hear* the growth of the tree. To prepare our ears, Rilke takes us as far back from the language of higher consciousness as he can to the world of primordial resonances, to the underworld of language in which agglutinations of sounds produce meaning. For instance, it is easy, even for an ear unattuned to German, to realize the connection between the words *Orpheus* and *Ohr* (ear). Orpheus, indeed, appears as a variation on the word *Ohr*, an extension of the ear. Similarly, the variations on the word-sound *Ohr* in the first quatrain operate as a beckoning sign for the Orphic metamorphosis and acoustic creation. Thus, the word *Ohr* resonates in 'O reine Ubersteigung' which, when pronounced, metamorphoses into *Ohr*, which transforms the ear itself into the *Ubersteigung*, that is, the crossing of the boundaries, while the association between *hoher* (taller) and *Ohr* prepares for the growth of the tree in the ear. If one adds to these resonances, the metamorphosis of the *o* of 'Ohr' into the *o* of 'Hören,' 'Geröhr,' and 'Gehör,' one soon realizes that the whole poem is built on echoes, that is, the purest of sounds, since an echo is a sound without a body. Relying on the Ovidian myth, one may add that it is a sound expressing feminine love.

In *Glas*, Derrida devises a new reading (and writing) that opposes the tendency to make an author an example of some truth or concept outside of himself or herself and of the author's work. As opposed to Sartre's interpretation of Genet's work as based on the concept of *vol* or theft, Derrida reads Genet's flowery discourse as 'flight' (another translation of the word *vol*). The phoneme *gl* which Derrida finds in Hegel's name, in the word 'glas,' and scattered throughout Genet's discourse allows Derrida to liberate signification from dialectics and conceptual thinking and to demonstrate how signification is an apparently random agglutination of semes according to the law of dissemination. The *gl* is a symptom of the combinatory process occurring within language and revealing what a text says unwittingly. The *gl* is a musical key because it is open to the sounds and rhythms of words, thus involving the ear as well as the eye in the act of writing. The *o* in Rilke's poem functions very much as the *gl* in *Glas*, which for Derrida demonstrates that 'la glu de l'aléa fait sens' ['the glue of chance makes sense' (GL 159b, 140b)]. The *o*, like the *gl*, produces signification by combining with other phonemes that it attracts. This model of signification follows the natural disseminative model of production and therefore befits the theme of this poem: the growth of a tree out of the ear. It is indeed, at the acoustic level, out of the *o* that the 'Ohr' and Orpheus arise. It is therefore out of the resonances heard in the silence of our ear that more than simple or universal meaning is produced in language.

This emphasis on the musical, acoustic element in language does not prevent Rilke from acknowledging the work of the eye in reading. As in Ponge's poetry, the letters themselves acquire substance. Thus, the letter *o* is also meant to be seen as a hieroglyphic representation of the cavern of the ear out of which the tree will grow. Similarly, in this poem the exclamation mark – physically a vertical line sprouting from a dot – seems to imitate the vertical growth of the tree from its seed in the ear, besides being acoustically just a breath. This presentation of the origin of art follows the organic growth of the plant, about which Goethe writes, 'The vertical tendency is manifest from the beginning of germination onward, for it is this tendency that enables the plant to take root and at the same time to lift itself upward.'[27]

As Marcuse points out, Orpheus is here associated with liberation, marked by a liberation of language from 'abstract' signification. In the sonnet we are reading, the Orphic song liberates animate & inanimate things from their physical and psychological entrapments. The animals leave their dens, the forest is freed (*gelöst*); the animals are liberated from cunning and desire, as well as from external noise (*Brüllen, Schrei, Geröhr*) so as to be filled with the silence of receptive hearing (*Hören*). It is this silent receptiveness that in turn transforms the ear from a simple hut into the silent temple in which the sacred gift can be worshipped.

This Orphic creation comes to resemble the Heideggerian *legein*, 'a laying,' gathering – also of course a reading – which is determined neither by vocalization (*phonē*), nor by signification (*semainein*), but which, unlike mere expression and signification, reaches into the realm of the primordial and essential ground of language. For Heidegger, 'Saying & talking occur essentially as the letting-lie-together before us of everything which, laid in unconcealment, comes to presence.'[28] Indeed, the Orphic creation is a revelation, in the sense of *Offenbarung,* a bringing into the open, an unfolding. In Rilke's poem, Orpheus's song allows the tree & the animals to appear out of a hearing which is a gathering together of self, a coming into oneself of self. It is dependent on a hearing that hardly has anything to do with the acoustic apparatus – which receives sounds from the outside – but is rather an inner hearing – the *Herz-Werk* of 'Wendung.' It is *Hören* linked with *Gehören.* Heidegger makes this link in his reading of Heraclitus: 'We are all ears when our gathering devotes itself entirely to harkening, the ears and the mere invasion of sounds being completely forgotten. . . . We have heard [*gehört*] when we belong [*gehören*] to the matter addressed.'[29]

Yet, as the poem shows, every gathering (*legein*) also involves a previous scattering. And linguistically there is in the poem a see-saw movement between scattering (freeing) and gathering (binding) of sounds and semes. Thus the 'steigen' of the tree becomes a 'Übersteigung,' a word growing out of the fusion of 'über' & 'steigen.' The word 'Übersteigung' can mean transcendence, but as such it belongs to the vocabulary of philosophy & abstraction. Rilke returns it to its organic origin in the growth of the tree, as well as in the overflowing of the ear. Similarly, the word 'Verschweigung' grows out of 'schweigen' expressed in the first part of line 3. The prefix *Ver* usually has a negative meaning; however, here the negativity is effaced by the end of the next line in 'Wandlung vor' – which enacts its own revelation of the metamorphosis.

Imitating Orpheus's power of creation through metamorphosis, and returning to the mythical world of Ovid, Rilke shows the link between the human and the vegetable by allowing an interpenetration of the two realms. Thus, in the next sonnet, it is not a tree that grows out of the ear, but a girl who has chosen the ear as her bed:

> *Und fast ein Mädchen wars und ging hervor*
> *aus diesem einigen Glück von Sang und Leier*
> *und gläntze klar durch ihre Frühlingsschleier*
> *und machte sich ein Bett in meinem Ohr.* (sw 1:731–32)

> *And it was almost a girl who, stepping from*
> *this single harmony of song and lyre,*
> *appeared to me through her diaphanous form*
> *and made herself a bed inside my ear.*
> (Mitchell, *Selected Poetry*, 229)

Once again, it is music that allows the apparition and the growth, but it is not only music, but rather the perfect unity of instrument and song. The process of creation presented here goes in the opposite direction: it is not a tree growing out of the ear, but a girl entering the ear and going to bed there. As in Proust, this poem shows the reciprocal relationship between the outside world and the receptive mind of the artist, as well as the necessary mixture of feminine and masculine in the creative mind.

Eventually, Orpheus himself becomes a flower. Not only is he associated with organic creation through song but, because he belongs to both worlds in Rilke's cosmology, he represents the flower's ability to appear in the world of light and to disappear into the underworld:

> *Erichtet keinen Denkstein. Laßt die Rose*
> *nur jedes Jahr zu seinen Gunsten blühn.*
> *Denn Orpheus ists. Seine Metamorphose*
> *in dem und dem. Wir sollen uns nicht mühn*
>
> *um andre Namen.* (sw 1:733)

> *Erect no gravestone to his memory; just*
> *let the rose blossom each year for his sake.*
> *For it is Orpheus. Wherever he has passed*
> *through this or that. We do not need to look*
>
> *for other names.* (Mitchell, *Selected Poetry,* 233)

The *Sonette an Orpheus* is not a lament about the disappearance and eventual death of Orpheus; it is a celebration of his creative power. In fact, as the myth tells us, Orpheus does not die, since his dismembered body lives on in the waters and the stars and his lyre keeps on singing. Moreover, as a flower, as a rose, Orpheus will never die; he will simply vanish momentarily, go back into concealment, as flowers must do. In this sonnet, Orpheus is not simply metamorphosed into a rose, he *is* a rose, and, what is even more important, rose is his name. This is why we need not erect a gravestone to his memory: each rose is his gravestone. He lives and is buried at the same time in every rose. And as a flower, Orpheus belongs to the world of dissemination (evident in the words 'Seine Metamorphose in dem und dem') and to the eternal cycle of death and rebirth.

As we already noted, Rilke's poetry attempts to resemble the wind, a breath, the kind of wind that caresses words, as the wind caressed Daphne. Sonnet 2.14 concentrates on this flight, which Rilke discovers in the natural world.

> *Siehe die Blumen, diese dem Irdischen treuen*
> *denen wir Schicksal vom Rande des Schicksals leihn, –*

aber wer weiß es! Wenn sie ihr Welken bereuen,
ist es an uns, ihre Reue zu sein.

Alles will schweben. Da gehn wir umher wie Beschwerer,
legen auf alles uns selbst, vom Gewichte entzückt;
o was sind wir den Dingen für zeherende Lehrer,
weil ihnen ewige Kindheit glückt.

Nähme sie einer ins innige Schlafen und schliefe
tief mit den Dingen – : o wie käme er leicht,
anders zum anderen Tag, aus der gemeinsamen Tiefe,

Oder er bliebe vielleicht; und sie blühten und priesen
ihn, den Bekehrten, der nun den Ihrigen gleicht,
allen den stillen Geschwistern in Winde der Wiesen.
(sw 1:760)

Look at the flowers, so faithful to what is earthly,
to whom we land fate from the border of fate.
And if they are sad about how they must wither and die,
perhaps it is our vocation to be their regret.

All things want to fly. Only we are weighted down by
    desire,
caught in ourselves and enthralled with our heaviness.
Oh what consuming, negative teachers we are
for them, while eternal childhood fills them with grace.

If someone were to fall into intimate slumber, and slept
deeply with Things – : how easily he would come
to a different day, out of the mutual depth.

Or perhaps he would stay there; and they would blossom
    and praise
their newest convert, who now is like one of them,
all those silent companions in the wind of the meadows.
(Mitchell, *Selected Poetry*, 247)

In this poem, as so often in Rilke's cosmology, there is a
'turning away' from the usual hierarchy of beings. What was

above is below, unless perhaps, through metamorphosis, there is no difference or separation between above and below – as this poem seems to intimate. At the bottom of the ladder are men; at the top, flowers, animals, and insects – what Rilke calls here 'Dinge' and in the Eighth Duino Elegy 'Seligkeit der kleinen Kreaturen' (bliss of the tiny creatures). Hence, in this poem, 'we' are exhorted to look to the bottom of the ladder and turn to flowers and things as teachers, turn into them, and be converted ('den Bekehrten') by them, because they are the beacons of our destiny and destination. In fact, the whole poem is based on a movement from top to bottom, from above the ground to below the ground, from outside to inside, as well as from one thing into its contrary.

Because flowers have retained their closeness to the earth, they know their destiny, they are their destiny: they come out of the earth and go back to it. Whereas man is always 'am Rande des Schicksals' (at the border of fate): he is external to his destiny, and destination (in the earth). Not only is man external to his destiny, but he projects it onto others, ironically onto flowers, which he uses as symbols of the ephemerality of his life. The rhyme 'leihn/sein' emphasizes man's presumptuous imposition on flowers of what he seems to know they are.

The next stanza develops the opposition between man's ignorance of his destination and the intuition of things, by concentrating on movement. Movement in nature is upward: 'alles will schweben': a soaring, a dissemination, a free scattering characterizes 'all things.' Indeed, in nature, there is always a movement upward: the plant grows upward, pollen is in flight. In contrast, 'our' movement is circular ('wir gehen umher') and seemingly without direction. If it has direction, it is always from ourselves to things. If in the previous stanza, man seemed to lend to things what they themselves are able to give or be, here man imposes himself on things ('legen auf alles uns selbst'). Things are light because they simply are, they are selfless; man on the contrary is weighty, full of self.

The last two stanzas point to a way out of the opposition and enact a descent into the depth of the earth: Rilke uses variations and qualifications of the word 'tief' to point to our destiny and destination in 'aus der gemeinsame Tiefe' (out of the mutual depth). This descent is still both a turning downward and inward, a movement into the underground of the earth as well as into the inner places of man's being. This movement is also a turning away from self to things: 'Nähme sie einer ins innigen Schlafen.'

The end of the poem expresses two possibilities: the fate of Orpheus who came back, and that of 'den stillen Geschwistern im Winde der Wiese,' the fate of Persephone, Eurydice, and Antigone, the ones who have become converted ('Bekehrten'), who have turned away from the world of light, and who keep showing us our destiny and destination in the calmness and silence of life under the meadow. It is not by chance that Rilke calls the inhabitants of the underground 'Geschwistern' (companions). As myth teaches us, it is the women who stay underground, whereas men are always called back. This staying is based on an absence of desire, on an intuitive knowledge that the separation between above and underneath is a construct of the mind. It entails possessing the intuitive knowledge of the flower that it will always reappear according to the vegetative cycle of death and rebirth. Rilke seems to have understood all this and this is why he usually associates flowers with women, especially mothers.

In both flowers and women Rilke sees the annihilation of the boundaries between inside and outside, the equation of the world within and the world without, as well as the reconciliation between death and life:

Die Frauen, in denen unmittelbar, fruchtbarer und vertrauensvoller das Leben verweilt und wohnt, müssen ja im Grunde reifere Menschen geworden sein, menschlichere Menschen als der leichte, durch die Schwere keiner leiblichen Frucht unter die Oberfläche des Lebens herabgezogene Mann, der, dünkelhaft und hastig, unterschätzt, was er zu lieben meint.

Women, in whom life lingers and dwells more immediately, more fruitfully, and more confidently, must surely become riper and more human in their depths than light easygoing man, who is not pulled down beneath the surface of life by the weight of any bodily fruit.[30]

If men – males – seem to be in the worst position of separateness, they can however learn from 'motherhood,' from the fruitfulness of women and flowers. For Rilke believes that there is motherhood in man – it is the motherhood achieved through the art of poetic creation:

Das tiefste Erleben des Schaffenden ist weiblich–: denn es ist empfangendes und gebärendes Erleben. Der Dichter Obstfelder hat einmal, da er von dem Gesichte eines fremden Mannes sprach, geschrieben: 'es war' (wenn er zu reden begann) 'als hätte er eine Frau innen in ihm Platz genommen'–; es schien mir, als paßte das auf jeden Dichter, der zu reden beginnt.

The deepest experience of the creative artist is feminine, for it is an experience of conceiving and giving birth. The poet Obstfelder once wrote, speaking of the face of a stranger: 'When he began to speak, it was as though a woman had taken a seat within him.' It seems to me that every poet has had this experience in beginning to speak.[31]

If it is through poetry that man can approach motherhood, not just any kind of art will do. The kind of mimetic art that translates the world will destroy the world, bind it. Only the Orphic kind of singing coming from the feminine unconscious will release and liberate the world and return it to the inner spaces of the heart – this is art as praise:

Auront le paradis ceux qui vantent les choses
car quel examen de félicité

que de refaire avec des paroles la rose
ou d'imiter de la pomme la belle prose!
Quelle universelle complicité!
(sw II:735, originally published in French)

Will attain paradise, those who praise things
indeed, what felicitous examination it is
to remake with words the rose
or to imitate of the apple the beautiful prose!
What universal complicity.

This praise is thus the only way the male artist has of making the world closer to himself, of being an accomplice to it, rather than its spectator or destroyer. It is only when the natural world ceases to be the object of observation, but becomes associated with its roots in the underworld that some kind of fertilizing encounter is possible. This descent into the underworld – to which the flower always seems to lead – uncovers an unknown world of strange metamorphoses repressed by a mimetic horizontal model which always has a tendency to come back to the same, to the father. As such, whether in Rilke or Proust, the descent into the nocturnal world points to the fact that neither the flower, nor language, nor art in general has ever been comfortable in the realm of reasoned vision, the one, the singular, but has always sprung from the interstices of their monuments and laws.

CHAPTER THREE

The Manufacture of
the Meadow

Francis Ponge

*How can a man have a sense of a thing if he does not have its
germ in himself? What I ought to understand must evolve or-
ganically within me, and what I seem to learn is nothing but
nourishment – stimulation of the organism.* – Novalis, *Pollen*

S ince it is difficult to remain underground for very
long – unless one is called Eurydice or Persephone –
I propose that we come back to the surface, to the
meadow. As Ponge's work *La Fabrique du pré* (1971) shows,
the meadow (*le pré*) is at the same time our end and our
beginning; it is where we begin and where we end.[1] Most of
the myths I have alluded to in the previous chapters start in
a meadow: it is the site where Persephone was playing with
her friends before being abducted by Pluto; it is where Eurydice was gathering flowers before being bitten by a serpent, it is the place where Alice falls asleep before undertak-
ing her adventures. As a 'garden,' it is the place where Eve
picked the fruit that caused the Fall. As such the meadow
seems to be a dangerous place, a place where seduction
occurs.

Like Ponge, one should perhaps first ask the question,
what is a meadow? What is a *pré*? If we begin with the
dictionary, we soon realize that the meadow is, by defini-

tion, an undefined and undefinable space. The definitions merely send us from one signifier to another, running the risk of falling into tautology. What dictionaries stress and agree upon are the composition of the 'pré' (it is made of grass) and its *telos* (it is meant to nourish animals).

French etymology brings up salient elements which Ponge, who anticipated our search, introduces and scatters in his poem. In the Littré we find out that *pré* used to be spelled 'prée' – & this spelling still prevails in some areas – since it comes from the Latin *prata*: 'Prée au féminin représente le pluriel neutre *prata* qui, suivant l'usage de la langue faisait des pluriels neutres des féminins singuliers' (Prée in the feminine represents the plural neuter *prata* which, according to linguistic usage, turns plural neuters into singular feminine nouns). Here we find a linguistic evolution from the neutral, to the feminine, and finally to the masculine, as well as a transformation of a plural into a singular. This etymology reveals the presence of sexuality in the meadow, the burial of the feminine under the masculine name, and the tension between the singularity of the name and the hidden plurality of its elements.

After this search, we still do not really know what a meadow is in French or in English. As in the case of the flower for Rousseau, or time for Augustine, we are left with saying that we know it when we see it. What seems to be missing is, if not an actual meadow, at least the meadow inscribed in our mind, the trace that a particular meadow we have seen has left in us. We have all seen a meadow sometime somewhere, but each meadow might be different. One cannot even be sure that one 'sees' a meadow: more likely one comes upon a meadow by chance. The meadow, then, has a relationship to chance, an unforeseen discovery that gives us pleasure and perhaps seduces us.

All this suggests that Ponge's task is impossible, since he wants to express 'the pré that I mean': 'le pré que je veux dire' means at the same time 'the meadow I want to express' and 'the meadow I mean,' that is, this particular meadow. This is why, among the illustrations that accompany the poems and various drafts, Ponge provides a photograph of the meadow he means, and situates it along the Lignon River at Chantegrenouille. The *pré* in the photograph is much more banal than the name it is associated with. The name 'Chantegrenouille' (Singfrog) introduces the idea that a meadow is not simply a stretch of grass, but that it is also associated with music and animal life. The *pré* is not simply something visual but also aural. Besides, the banality of the *pré* in the photograph seems to emphasize Ponge's purpose of leaving behind any idyllic, pastoral, or romantic style of representation in order to present the *pré* as part of our ordinary world, a world in which twentieth-century individuals still must live. But this is only one illustration out of many. All the other plates have something to do with a meadow: they are all representations of meadows. Each adds one element to the previous one so as to create a more comprehensive mental image of the *pré*; they all emphasize the feelings associated with the *pré*. Jean-léon Gérôme's painting *After the Masked Ball* retrieves and illustrates the dictionary example of the 'pré aux clercs,' a place in Saint Germain des prés where students used to converse and engage in duels, so that the saying remained: 'aller au pré' (to go to the meadow) means to engage in a duel. The *pré* can be dangerous, then, and linked to various kinds of seduction. The main temptation in the *pré* is that it invites us to lie down, as Marc Chagall's painting *The Poet Lying Down* implies. It is thus a place of rest, but also a place of death. As Ponge's notes to 'Le Pré' suggest, first one lies on it, and soon one is lying under it.

What all of Ponge's illustrations show is that the *pré* is a bounded area, sometimes separated by fences, always bordered by trees, a river, rocks. As such it defines itself by what it is not, by what it is between, and by its fragmentation. We are starting to realize that the meadow has very little to do with the natural world; it is rather a cultural, psychological, and artistic *topos,* which Ponge attempts to return to the natural world. He tries to motivate this fairly empty signifier by rooting it back in nature, and thus not by describing it or defining it, but by attempting to 'make' it. Indeed, it is useless to try to find a definition of the word *pré* or 'meadow' in a botanical dictionary. The closest one gets to it is a definition of the 'grass family,' which includes 'seven thousand species' ranging from 'low growing herbaceous plants' to some (maize, sugar, cane) which grow ten to twelve feet in height, and a few (bamboo) which grow to be trees.'[2] Some grass species are self-pollinated and others are pollinated by the wind. As such, they depend on themselves or on chance.

Under the entry *pré* in the Littré, Ponge found another significant definition, that of the prefix *pré,* meaning 'before,' 'anterior,' and which appears in endless combinations – even in its own definition. This connection between the linguistic *pré* and the natural *pré* made Ponge realize the anteriority of both the *pré* and language: both have started before us, both precede us. Hence the urge of his poetry to return to the origin of language, to the oldest language & to the origin of the *pré,* which is the field of references par excellence, the living world, the meadow. As a natural space, the *pré,* or the vegetable realm in general, precedes humankind's appearance on the earth. Indeed, evolutionary botanists explain how plants developed before animals and humans, who could not have survived without them. Similarly, in the Bible, God, after separating the skies from the waters, and before populating either, caused vegetation to grow on the earth, and it is on this earth covered with plants bearing seeds that He placed Adam and Eve.

It is back to this original paradise that the first stanza of Ponge's poem takes us. It is also a time before language fell into the discursive languages of reason and logic, a time when language was still praise – praise in response to the glory of created things:

La louange aussitôt s'enfle dans notre gorge.
Nous croyons être au paradis. (FP lines 3–4)

Then praise at once swells in our throats.
We feel we are in paradise. (MP 225)

This paradise, however, is not lost, it can be retrieved, each time Nature prepares a *pré* for us – which she does endlessly – and every time we allow it to appear and grow through our praise. Indeed, for Ponge, the *pré* is there, it is prepared for us as a gift by nature, but it is our duty to make it appear. In his notes to 'Le Pré,' Ponge writes: 'Notre devoir dès lors, notre merci nous invite à la parole. . . . Telle est notre façon d'être et de l'en louer' (FP 250) [Our duty from here on, our thanks, invites us to speech. . . . Our way of being is to praise it (the *pré,* (MP 155)]. If the language that allows the *pré* to manifest itself is not the discursive language of logic and reason, it is because the *pré* rebukes logic and a language that has separated itself from nature. As Ponge tells us, the *pré* is 'une façon d'être,' a way of being. Ponge returns here to the original meaning of the Greek 'being,' the original being which, Heidegger suggests, we have fallen away from: 'Being in the sense of *physis* is the power that emerges.' This original being as *physis* is not opposed to becoming: 'becoming as "emerging" belongs to physis.'[3] This is why in his poem Ponge prefers the dynamism of speech to the finished and static nature of painting to represent the *pré.* The kind of speech Ponge has in mind is the Heideggerian *legein,* that is, a gathering, a collecting, a reading, which allows truth to emerge:

Ils naissent autrement
Ils sourdent [emerge] de la page.

Préparons donc la page où puisse aujourd'hui naître
Une vérité qui soit verte. (FP lines 13–17)

They are born another way
They well up from the page.

So let us prepare the page where may be born today
A verity that is verdant. (MP 225)

All the poet can do, then, is to prepare himself for the emergence of being as *physis,* to read what nature has already
proposed (said), or, as Ponge wishes, to let nature speak
through him. This is the tour de force that 'Le Pré' is supposed to perform. It will require some magic, a magic often
associated with herbs, and a return to their roots.

In an interview with Philippe Sollers, Francis Ponge
comments on his birth and roots in the south of France,
namely in Nîmes where he was born and in Avignon where
he lived. 'Il est certain que je suis une herbe ou une bran-
chette, une feuille d'un arbre de ces régions et que cela m'a
détérminé' [I am undoubtedly a blade of grass or a little
branch, a leaf from a tree of those regions, and that determined me].[4] Even though this is only a metaphor, and a
common one, it is characteristic of Ponge to use botanical
analogies to refer to himself as a 'poet' and to his poems.
Given the abundance of such analogies as well as the number of poems devoted to flowers, trees, and grass, one might
argue that, among the 'choses' of 'le monde muet [qui] est
notre seule patrie' [the silent world (which) is our only
homeland], the natural things, & more precisely the flora,
occupy a privileged position in his work. If Ponge's writing
does indeed take 'le parti (pris) des choses,' and celebrates
the singularity and multiplicity of animate & inanimate
things, there is in his work, however, a marked predilection for the vegetable realm which prepares the ground for
writing.

Thus, in several texts from *Le Parti pris des choses* (*The
Voice of Things*), Ponge expresses the congruence between
vegetation and the medium of poetry. In 'Faune et flore,' the
flora is presented as being in the same predicament as the
poet, especially a poet such as Ponge: 'Malgré tous leurs
efforts pour "s'exprimer," ils ne parviennent jamais qu'à

répéter un million de fois la même expression, la même feuille . . . la même note, le même mot, la même feuille' ['Despite all their efforts to "express themselves," they only manage to repeat a million times over the same expression, the same leaf . . . the same note, the same word, the same leaf'].[5] The correlation between the vegetable world and the poet is even more clearly expressed in the following remark, also from 'Faune et flore': 'Où qu'ils naissent, si cachés qu'ils soient, ils ne s'occupent qu'à accomplir leur expression: ils se préparent, ils s'ornent, ils attendent qu'on vienne les lire' (PPC 68) ['Wherever they grow, however hidden they are, their only activity is the accomplishment of their expression: they prepare themselves, adorn themselves, wait for someone to come and read them' (VT 64)].

The vegetable world, as it is presented in this text, functions at the same time as a mirror for the poet and for the poem. It is a reflection of the poet since, like him, all it has at its disposal is the same old medium of expression, the same old leaf. In the same way that plants can only produce what seems to be the same leaf over and over again, the poet can only produce the same words over and over again. And for Ponge, they are the same old words, worn out by centuries of use and abuse. On the other hand, the accomplishment of the flora is, like a poem, something meant to be read. The purpose of the vegetable world vis-à-vis its medium is congruent with the purpose of the poet vis-à-vis his linguistic medium: to realize it, to perfect it, and even more significant, to give it shape, a form: 'Oisifs, ils passent leur temps à compliquer leur forme, à parfaire dans le sens de la plus grande complication d'analyse leur propre corps' (PPC 68) ['Idle creatures, they pass the time complicating their own form, perfecting their own body in terms of greatest analytical complication' (VT 64)]. Moreover, contrary to the oral mode of animal expression, the flora expresses itself in writing. Not only is the expression of the flora written, it is written once & for all, as if paradoxically inscribed in stone: 'L'expression des végétaux est écrite, une fois pour toutes. Pas moyen d'y revenir, repentirs impossibles: pour se corriger, il faut ajouter. Corriger un texte écrit, et *paru,* par des appendices, et ainsi de suite' (PPC 70) ['Plant expression is written, once & for all. No way of retracting, no repenting possible: correcting means adding. A text written and *published* is corrected by appendices, and still more appendices' (VT 66)]. If one did not know that this passage applies to the flora, one might be tempted to read it as a description of Ponge's poetics: a series of corrections, additions, repetitions, always apparently of the same thing.

This vegetable accomplishment provides the subject as well as the form of *La Fabrique du pré,* one of the best examples in Ponge's work of the organic nature of writing, based on a 'rhizomatic' relationship between the botanical and the literary. *La Fabrique du pré* is a particular kind of book which, in its formal arrangement, parallels its subject matter, and more generally reproduces the theme of Ponge's work. Ponge remarks that what he wanted to achieve through his writing was something like Lucretius's *De Rerum Natura,* which Ponge would rather call 'De Varietate Rerum.' The apparently finished poem 'Le Pré' constitutes only a small part of the book which presents the variety of shapes, colors, and dimensions through which the natural world appeals to our senses. Through its peculiar format, the book is no longer an abstract term referring to some reading material, instead, it has been transmuted into a sensual object presented in its multidimensional facets. Indeed, the pages of the book are of different colors and textures. Together with the texture, the typography also varies: capitals, italics, manuscripts, dictionary entries, and diary entries form a panoply of the different shapes that words and things can take. If one adds to this series the reproductions of paintings, tapestries, and miniatures, and musical partitions as well as plates from a botanical dictionary, the book as a whole appears as an encyclopedia of the various complementary representational forms that constitute the precarious unity of the *pré*.

As in most of his other poems, Ponge attempts not so much to describe the object, albeit in a new way, as to allow the object to speak through him, through his words. He does not so much want to express the object as to give the object an opportunity to express itself. However, as we have already noted in the preliminary remarks from 'Faune et flore,' the flora is already a mode of expression and signification: 'Cette modification de la sempiternell feuille signifie certainement quelque chose' (PPC 68) ['This modification of the perpetual leaf certainly means something' (VT 64)].

If there is already expression and signification in the natural world, consequently the task of the poet becomes that of a translator. It is significant that Ponge's definition of his task vis-à-vis the world of silent things is similar to the reciprocal relationship between the text and its translator in Walter Benjamin's 'Die Aufgabe des Übersetzers' (The Task of the Translator). In Benjamin's dialectical model, the text is a *Gabe* (a gift) which constitutes an *Aufgabe* (a debt, an indebtedness, a duty) on the part of the translator. Similarly, as the first stanza of 'Le Pré' indicates, the natural world is a gift, the given of Ponge's poetry, but also that which dictates his duty as a poet. The purpose of the translation of a text or of the text of nature is also similar: a reconciliation between the different languages of the world, a unity within multiplicity and a celebration of language in Benjamin, a reconciliation of mind and nature, a celebration of the adequation between the language of humans and the language of nature in Ponge. The task of the poet is, indeed, to translate the language of nature into the language of humans, to translate the natural *pré* into the linguistic *pré*, and thus to enact the passage from expression to communication. In *Signéponge/Signsponge*, Derrida suggests that the 'thing' – here the meadow – is the 'other' uttering a silent demand in and to the self:

La chose serait donc l'autre, l'autre-chose qui me donne un ordre ou m'adresse une demande impossible, intransigeante, insatiable, sans échange, et sans transaction, sans contrat possible. Sans un mot, sans me parler, elle s'adresse à moi seul dans mon irremplaçable singularité, dans ma solitude aussi.

Thus the thing would be the other, the other thing which gives me an order or addresses an impossible, intransigent, insatiable demand to me, without an exchange & without a transaction, without a possible contract. Without a word, without speaking to me, it addresses itself to me, to me alone in my irreplaceable singularity, in my solitude as well.[6]

There is, as Derrida perceived, a relationship between the thing and the poet: the thing calls, demands, the poet responds without any concern for any reward other than, perhaps, the birth of a poem.

If the poet is forced to be a translator, it is because we do not understand the language that natural things use to speak to us. Thus in 'Tentative orale,' Ponge comments on the attempt of a forest to express itself:

Pour moi, je ne doute pas qu'une forêt veuille vous parler; elle veut vous montrer son coeur. Au printemps (cela se trouve comme cela), elle n'y tient plus: après ce silence de plusieurs mois elle vomit du vert, elle s'exprime, elle pousse des feuilles, des tiges; sur ces tiges des feuilles; brusquement, elle s'épaissit, quelle profusion! Cela est magnifique, elle progresse, croit atteindre à la communication. . . . Or, quelle était son intention? Elle voulait nous montrer son coeur, jamais, elle ne nous l'a mieux caché. Jamais il ne nous a paru plus impénétrable.

For my part, I never doubted that a forest wants to talk to us; it wants to show us its heart. In spring (that's how it goes), it can't wait: after a silence of several months it throws up green; it expresses itself, it grows leaves, stems; suddenly, it becomes thicker, what a profusion! It is magnificent, it progresses, it imagines it has achieved communication. . . . Well, what was its intention? It wanted to show us its heart, never has it managed to conceal it better. Never has it appeared as unreachable.[7]

As I already intimated, however, the spoken word is not going to be the medium through which the poet can express the heart of the forest or the poet's own. Through speech, the poet could only do the same thing as the forest, conceal its heart and his own, as the rest of 'Tentative orale' reveals. Moreover, speech is fallen discourse, the kind of discourse that has separated itself from nature, from nature and being – what Hélène Cixous calls 'un discours qui parle de haut' [a discourse which speaks from on high]. Penetrating into the heart of natural things requires writing, the kind of inscription that will ensure the survival of the object, the poem, and the poet.

As has been pointed out by the abundant criticism of his work, Ponge's poetry, besides being about objects, is primarily about itself. Critics interested in Ponge as a metapoet quote his formula 'Le parti pris des choses égale compte tenu des mots' (Taking the side of things is taking account of words) & comment on the relationship between 'l'épaisseur des choses' (the depth of things) et 'l'épaisseur sémantique des mots,' (the semantic depth of words) as well as on his attempt to achieve a congruence between the two spheres. But in so doing, they reestablish the gap between words and world which Ponge attempts to bridge, and deny the singularity of his poetry. Thus, in *Entretiens,* Philippe Sollers claims that 'le texte se désigne lui-même et ne parle finalement que de lui' [the text designates itself, & finally comments only on itself]. Similarly, Robert Greene asks the following rhetorical question: 'Is "Le pré" in fact concerned not so much with the meadow but with the limitations and real possibilities of language?'[8] Ponge's adequation, however, is not to be understood too literally; it is the kind of equivalence that is supposed to allow both language and the 'thing' to 'be described,' to exist as separate elements. In this connection between world and word, what is offered to the reader is the copulation and *jouissance* out of which the world and the word, each retaining its own particular and separate identity, are born anew. Hence, the scruples and hesitations in Ponge's poetry: hesitations to begin, to continue, and especially to end what can only be a process, a dynamics, and must remain so for fear that the object might be engulfed by the word, and thus disappear entirely.

This adequation between words and things is not as purely mimetic as one might think; it is rather 'rhizomatic,' in the sense in which Deleuze and Guattari use the word in *Mille plateaux*.[9] The rhizome – whose roots ramify horizontally – suits Ponge's researches in the dictionary, especially his rapprochement between roots that do not seem to be etymologically (and thus genealogically) related (such as *pré, près,* and *prêt* in *La Fabrique du pré*). Besides, Deleuze and Guattari's description of the rhizomatic relationship between heterogeneous systems can explain the relationship between things and words in Ponge's poetry because it provides a botanical model of signification that surpasses the traditional equivalence of signifier and signified.

Ponge is, of course, not so naive as to think that there could be an equivalence between words and things, or to believe that words can duplicate things. Besides, if such a possibility existed, it would prove to mean the death of the 'thing,' if not the destruction of the pleasure of writing and reading. Renée Riese Hubert recognizes that 'since the poet's goal is expression, writing, words, he carefully refrains from asserting any kind of mimesis.' Her appreciation and knowledge of Ponge's poetry as well as her affinity with the visual world of illustrations enable her to acknowledge the play and fascination of Ponge's poetry: 'As usual with Ponge, we witness a quest for, and a groping transformation into, writing.' In Ponge's poetry, the word and the thing 'font rhizome en tant qu'hétérogènes' [form a rhizome, as heterogeneous elements].[10]

It is in this sense that the relationship between the natural *pré* and the poetic *pré* makes sense; it is only if language and the external world are allowed to remain heterogeneous spheres that Ponge's poetry can be a celebration of both language *and* nature. To forget the heterogeneity of these two spheres is precisely what Ponge describes in *Pour un Malherbe* as

le danger de l'esprit absolu. Celui d'oublier que la représentation esthétique d'un objet ou d'un sentiment du monde extérieur se fait positivement dans un autre monde, avec d'autres éléments, avec une autre matière. Concernant la littérature, elle se fait dans la matière verbale. Il est absurde, sans doute, à la limite, de vouloir soumettre une matière d'un tel ordre aux lois d'une matière toute différente.

the danger of the absolute spirit. The tendency to forget that the aesthetic representation of an object or of a feeling emanating from the outside world is achieved positively in another world, with other elements, with another material. As for literature, it is made out of verbal matter. It is undoubtedly absurd to expect to subjugate a material of such an order to the laws of a completely different material.[11]

This passage from one order to another, if it is to respect the integrity of each, necessitates the kind of translation that I have just described.

This kind of translation, as it celebrates both language and the thing named, ensures not only the survival of both, but also that of human beings themselves. This translation is indeed the human task par excellence since it gives back to us our true place in the universe: 'Il suffit d'abaisser notre prétention à dominer la nature et d'élever notre prétention à en faire physiquement partie, pour que la réconciliation ait lieu' [One only needs to lower one's pretensions to dominate nature and to raise one's pretensions to be a physical part of it, if one wants the reconciliation to take place].[12] This necessary relationship between humankind and nature is not on Ponge's part a sentimental return to a prelapsarian state of innocence, rather it derives from our very being. An individual, as a subject, is a lack: one needs an object in order to *be* (oneself). Without an object (the external world), there can be no verb, especially no verb 'to be' – the copula between us and the outside world – and hence no language other than the tautological and solipsistic Cartesian *cogito:*

L' homme est un drôle de corps, qui n'a pas son centre de gravité en lui-même. Notre âme est transitive. Il lui faut un object, qui l'affecte, comme son complément direct, aussitôt. Il s'agit du rapport le plus grave (non du tout de l'avoir, *mais de* l'être). *L'artiste, plus que tout autre homme, en reçoit la charge, accuse le coup.*

Man is a strange body, which does not have its center of gravity within himself. Our soul is transitive. It needs an object, which affects it, like its direct object, immediately. This is the most serious relationship (not at all that of the having *but of* the being). *The artist, more so than any other man, takes up this task, acknowledges this responsibility.*[13]

This definition is significant because it presents the poet as the Verb, the copula between the subject-man and the object-nature, as the necessary link by which we come into being.

The very title, *La Fabrique du pré,* expresses a willed ambiguity between subject and object, which stresses the reciprocal and specular relationship between the poet and the *pré.* Thus, in the title, the *pré* can either be the subject or the object of the making, and of course it is both, since the *pré* is also that which 'fera mon propos d'aujourd'hui' [will be my proposition for today]. The use of *fera* in this sentence, even though as colloquial as *sera* would be, stresses the reciprocal relationship between the poem as a linguistic material and the *pré* as a geophysical matter. The rapprochement between the physical *pré* & the linguistic *pré* depends on an unveiling of the ramifications of meanings hidden in words. For instance, as I noted earlier, 'le pré que je veux dire' has to be read idiomatically as 'the *pré* I mean,' that is, as a demonstrative pointing to the actual *pré*, but also literally as 'the *pré* I want to express.' If there is to be any coincidence between the natural *pré* and the linguistic *pré*, between 'the *pré* I mean' and 'the *pré* I want to express,' the poem must reflect the tension between the plurality and multiplicity of the blades of grass on the one hand, and the unity and singularity of the *pré*, on the other. The use of the word *fabrique* designates this dynamic tension: *fabrique* can refer both to the construction of an edifice (unity) and to the members constituting a factory (multiplicity). In *De Rerum Natura*, Lucretius establishes a similar relationship between creation in the natural world under an endless combination and transformation of elements and the various combinations of letters and words in a poem. The lives of plants, animals, humans, and poems depend on an endless process of combining, recombining and reshuffling, which creates a unity out of multiplicity. And the tour de force of the poem will be to render visible, audible and significant this multiple unity, to create a unity that will preserve this multiplicity.

This is why, at the beginning of the poem, we are confronted with a strange statement – especially coming from Ponge – that the *pré* lends itself better to language than to painting. This privileging of language as a medium of representation over painting should, of course, surprise us from someone who values painting as much as Ponge does, all the more so that one is dealing here with the subject of painting par excellence: a landscape, a meadow. Even though the visual element of the *pré* is important, the *pré* that Ponge wants to offer us is not addressed only to our eyes: it is not 'un plat à nos yeux servi.' Ponge is here playing on the different meanings and dimensions of the word 'plat,' which can mean a dish (especially followed by the word *servi*), but also a flat surface. Even though, later in the poem, the *pré* becomes 'un aliment' (food), the *pré* is not supposed to be a ready-made dish meant for our passive consumption; nor is it supposed to be the flat surface that painting would present.

If this definition of the representation of the *pré* by painting sounds naive and reductive, as if Ponge thought that painting cannot represent variety within unity, or relief and texture, it is only because painting lacks an essential element that Ponge associates with language and with the vegetable world, namely sound. Compared to language, then, painting remains somehow one-dimensional, whereas the linguistic model, like the vegetable model, is three-dimensional, since it comprehends the visual (the signs on the page), the musical (the phonetic sounds), and signification, which appears as the synthesis of the first two. And for Ponge, as expressed in 'Végétation,' the vegetable world is 'une tapisserie à trois dimensions' (PPC 74) ['a three-dimensional tapestry' VT 68)].

If in other texts Ponge compares the medium at the poet's disposal to the poverty of the painter who would have at his disposal only one color, here color appears as a poor and pedestrian means compared to the three-dimensional realm of language.[14] Thus, 'Prendre un tube de vert, l'étaler sur la page, / ce n'est pas faire un pré' (FP line 11) [To take a tube of green and spread it on the page / Will fail to make a *pré* (MP 225)]. Why? Ponge answers himself in the third stanza:

> *Parce qu'il s'agit plus d'une façon d'être*
> *Que d'un plat à nos yeux servi,*
> *La parole y convient plutôt que la peinture*
> *Qui n'y suffirait nullement* (FP lines 7–10)

> Since we are concerned here more with a way of being
> Than with a platter served up before our eyes,
> Speech is more suitable than paint
> Which would never do (MP 225)

Painting, with its particular medium, cannot make a *pré,* cannot create a *pré;* it can only represent it as made, as finished. Only language, especially the French language, with its dynamic relationship of accents, can give birth to the *pré,* and represent the process of this birth, its dynamic and particular way of being. Interestingly, the French language displays a subtle relationship between speech and writing: accents are both visible and phonetic marks, which subtly make and alter signification, as can be seen in Ponge's game about the relationship between *pré, près,* and *prêt.* Such vocal and visual differences can better recreate the subtle differences between the blades of grass of the meadow. In the preparatory notes to 'Le Pré,' Ponge plays on the diacritical marks of the French language, especially on the 'accent aigu' in the word 'pré' which he sees as 'une herbe,' as 'une goutellette liquide' ['drop of water'], as 'une virgule' and 'vergette' ['comma' and 'little penis'], as 'un point de rosée' ['a dew drop'], as well as 'l'oiseau' which 'de son accent aigu y égratigne le ciel en sens inverse de l'écriture (et donc de la signification)' ['the bird (which) with his acute accent scratches the sky in the opposite direction of writing (and thus of signification)'] (FP 201, 202, 254) (MP 24, 25, 165). This game allows Ponge to bring writing closer to the natural object at hand, to make us visualize both language and the *pré,* as well as to stress the dynamic variety of the *pré.*

What strikes us at the beginning of the poem is the association of the making of the *pré* not so much with writing as with speech. In fact, the poem is presented as a speech given in front of an audience, as the line 'Qui fera mon propos d'aujourd'hui' intimates. Again, as readers of Ponge, we can express our surprise at such an apparent privileging of speech, since we know that Ponge distrusts conversations and dislikes lectures. It seems, however, that Ponge wants to express the singularity of the *pré* in an impromptu manner which would resemble the directness, transience, and unfinished quality of speech rather than through the finished quality of writing. We know, as well as Ponge does, that this directness, this improvised quality is impossible to sustain in writing, unless the boundaries between speech and writing can be crossed. The task of the poet will be to attempt to maintain this unfinished quality of speech, and thus to repeat the endless birth and rebirth of the *pré*. To express this dynamic birth of the *pré,* all the poet can do is eventually to prepare himself and the page: 'Préparons donc la page où puisse aujourd'hui naître / Une vérité qui soit verte' (FP lines 16–17) [So let us prepare the page where may be born today / A verity that is verdant (MP 225)]. Moreover, all the poet can do is prepare himself and us for something that nature has already prepared for him, for us, in advance. In this sense, the 'propos' of the poet does not necessarily link the poem to speech; rather it presents the poem as a response to the proposal of nature expressed in the first lines of 'Le Pré': 'Que parfois la Nature, à notre réveil, nous propose / Ce à quoi justement nous étions disposés, / La louange aussitôt s'enfle dans notre gorge' (FP lines 1–3) [Should Nature at times, on our awakening, propose to us / The very thing to which we were disposed / Then praise at once swells in our throat (MP 225)]. In this sense, therefore, the 'propos d'aujourd'hui' appears as an immediate response to, and celebration of, what nature proposes to us.

The *pré* in Ponge's poem is indeed something that na-ture – which Ponge finds both inside us, as our 'nature,' and outside us, as 'Nature' – has always prepared for us, and prepared us for. The *pré* is 'pré-paré,' both anterior to us and before us today, as well, of course, as always adorned (*paré*). It is 'proposé' but also 'ce à quoi nous étions disposés,' and thus both a past and a future, which at our awakening we are supposed to experience as a present (also a gift), since the *pré* is already present in 'présent.'

Should it surprise, therefore, if 'Le Pré' cannot begin, or if the poet cannot begin the *pré,* since the *pré* has always already begun without him? The *pré* in Ponge's poem is associated with time, which is another reason why the medium of language is better suited to its creation than the spatial medium of painting. The mixture of past, present, and future characteristic of the natural *pré* is reflected in the mixture of tenses that pervades the poem, and is already expressed in the first lines that I quoted earlier: 'Voilà comme il en *fut* du pré que *je veux dire* / Qui *fera* mon propos *d'aujourd'hui*' (my emphasis). This mixture of times and tenses, rather than indicating that the *pré* and its composition belong to the realm of timeless universality, points to the relationship between the natural *pré* and the linguistic *pré*. As a natural organism, the *pré* is always in process, always already there, but also always to come.

Thus, in the apparently finished version of the poem on the brown pages called 'Le Pré,' there is a 'prose' fragment, in parentheses and symbolically separated from the rest of the poem by dotted lines (a river?), which tells us about a passage that should be included in this particular space. If it is to express any congruence with the *pré*, Ponge's poem will have to resist closure, and present the *pré* as always to come. This prose passage significantly deals with the rapprochement between the physical birth of the *pré* out of its diverse natural elements and the linguistic birth of the *pré* out of the elements of writing. Thus Ponge writes: 'Je tacherai d'expliquer, je dis bien d'expliquer, deux ou trois choses, et d'abord que si le pré dans notre langue, représente une des plus importantes et primordiales notions qui soient, il en est de même sur le plan physique (géophysique)' (FP lines 78–83) ['I will try to explain, I do mean explain, two or three things, and first of all that if the *pré*, in French, represents one of the most important and primordial notions that exist, the same is true on the physical (geophysical) level'] (MP 228). The word 'explain,' which Ponge stresses through its repetition, is not a word commonly found in poetry, not even in Ponge's poetry. It reveals the didactic quality of the poem which, at times, reads like an ecological treatise reminding us that we are part of nature. Linguistically, *pré* is one of the most original words, as it is at the origin of so many combinations and meanings. Similarly, in the physical realm, the origin of the *pré* is one of the most essential elements: 'l'eau,' a shapeless substance to which the vegetable world gives a form. It is in this sense also that the *pré* is 'une métamorphose de l'eau.' Going back further in the natural birth of the *pré*, at the origin of the *pré* is water, and at the origin of water is the original thunder: 'L'orage originel aura longtemps parlé' (FP line 101) ['The original storm has spoken at length' (MP 229)]. If the liquid element of water links the creation of the *pré* with the original element of writing, ink, then the reference to thunder links its creation with sounds, thus again showing the interrelation of speech and writing in the creation of the *pré*.

The connection between the poetic birth of the *pré* and the geophysical process goes much further in this passage, even though only the physical process is detailed.

Il s'agit en vérité d'une métamorphose de l'eau, laquelle, au lieu de s'évaporer directement à l'appel du feu, en nuages, choisit ici, se liant à la terre et en passant par elle, c'est-à-dire par les restes pétris du passé des trois règnes et en paticulier par les granulations les plus fines du minéral, réimprégnant en somme le cendrier universel, de donner renaissance à la vie sous la forme la plus élémentaire, l'herbe: élémentarité, alimentarité. (FP lines 83–92)

It actually involves a metamorphosis of water, which instead of evaporating directly, at the summons of fire, into clouds, chooses here, by linking itself to earth and passing through it, that is to say, through the kneaded remains of the three kingdoms and particularly through the finest grains of the mineral, in short reimpregnating the universal ashtray, to give renascence to life in its most elementary form, grass: elementarity, alimentarity. (MP 228–29)

At the physical level, the *pré* is thus born, and reborn, out of the connection between water and the remnants of the past mineral elements. The temporal cycle and natural recycling are obvious in this process: it is out of the 'cendrier universel,' the remnants of past lives, including dead leaves, dead wood, and minerals that the elementary single blade of grass that makes up the *pré* is born, and perpetually reborn. Moreover, the cycle starts again as the 'élémentarité' of the grass blade becomes in turn the 'alimentarité' of animals. In this endless process, the grass is the food of the cattle, which produce milk, the food of people and animals; while in turn, the grass becomes the seasoning of the beef, the food of humanity. It is in this sense that the *pré*, first at the physical level, but also at the poetic level, connects all the elements of the cosmic creation: mineral, vegetable, animal, and human, to include as well the atmospheric (the skies, the clouds, the thunder).

The reader is invited to pursue the second term of the comparison and make the connection between the physical birth of the *pré* & the linguistic birth of the *pré*. In *La Fabrique du pré,* perhaps even more than in his other poems, Ponge stresses the materiality of language and of writing. The page, the ink, the typography, the accents are meant to be experienced by the reader as objects involved in a cosmological symbiosis resembling that of natural production. The poem, like the *pré,* is thus born out of the coming together of the ink and the page. The page, here, is not simply the abstract space on which the poet writes, it is the actual and physical material that finds its origin in the vegetable realm, and of course, it is brown like the earth. Moreover, the poem is a response to a speechless and originary calling in the poet, a homologue of the external thunder.

As Ponge stresses, his poetry is born out of an emotion that the outside world provokes in him:

Vous savez que ce qui me porte ou me pousse, m'oblige à écrire, c'est l'émotion que procure le mutisme des choses qui nous entourent. Peut-être s'agit-il d'une sorte de pitié, de sollicitude, enfin j'ai le sentiment d'instances muettes de la part des choses qui solliciteraient de nous qu'enfin l'on s'occupe d'elles et les parle.

You know that what entices me, or pushes me, obliges me to write is the emotion provoked by the silence of the things that surround us. Whether it is some kind of pity or solicitude, I have the feeling of silent demands on the part of things which would require of us that we start taking care of them and giving them expression.[15]

Like the *pré*, which Ponge describes in the diary entries as 'une étendue de vert qui jaillit lentement en appel anonyme ou réponse à la pluie' ['an expanse of green that shoots forth slowly in anonymous appeal or response to the rain'], Ponge's poem is a response to the silent and anonymous calling of the *pré* (FP 220, MP 79).

Moreover, the birth of the *pré* out of the connection between rain & earth (ink & paper) finds its homologue in the copulation between words & things. To succeed, this copulation has to be a copulation of equals. Only in that case can the disappearance of the duality between words and things be achieved, and can a return to primeval nomination be attained. This is why Ponge's poetry is not 'poetic' in the traditional sense of the word, especially 'Le Pré' which presents itself as a lecture. Ponge does not like being called a 'poet': he considers poetry as an imposture, compared to the 'nomination originelle' that his writing attempts to recover. This original naming would be the kind of naming in which things are given a voice, in which things are allowed to come into their being:

En somme, les choses sont, déjà, autant mots *que choses et, réciproquement, les mots* déjà, *sont* autant choses que mots. *C'est leur copulation, que réalise l'écriture (véritable, ou parfaite): C'est l'orgasme qui en résulte, qui provoque notre jubilation. Il s'agit de les faire* rentrer *l'un dans l'autre: de ne plus voir* double: *que les apparences se confondent (exactement).*

In fact, things are, already, as much words *as things and, reciprocally, words are,* already, as much things as words. *It is their copulation that (true and perfect) writing achieves: it is the orgasm that results from it that provokes our jubilation. It is a matter of making them* penetrate *into one another: it is a question of no longer seeing* double: *it is a question of letting appearances merge (exactly).*[16]

If words are already things & things already words, Ponge's translation of things into words can only be a repetition, a pleonastic act, as he calls it in *La Fabrique du pré*. Besides, this birth resulting from the copulation of words and things is always, by definition a rebirth, and the making (of the *pré*) is always a remaking, a reparation of the originary unity and equality between world and word:

Seule la littérature (et seule dans la littérature, celle de la description – par opposition à celle de l'explication – : parti pris des choses, dictionnaire phénoménologique, cosmogonie) permet de jouer le grand jeu: de refaire le monde, à tous les sens du mot refaire, *grâce au caractère à la fois concret et abstrait, intérieur et extérieur du* VERBE, *grâce à son épaisseur sémantique.*

Only literature (and only in literature, the literature of description – in contrast to the literature of explication – : the side of things, phenomenological dictionary, cosmogony) allows one to play one's card: to re-make the world, in all the senses of the word re-make, *thanks to the similarly concrete and abstract, internal and external character of the* VERB, *thanks to its semantic depth.*[17]

This remaking of the world, which is also a remaking or reparation of words, is here linked with the dictionary, a key element in Ponge's writing. The dictionary, and especially Littré, can be seen as an equivalent of what Ponge calls 'le cendrier universel' in *La Fabrique du Pré*. Each is an aggregate mass of the remnants, roots, citations from the past writers and grass, out of which Ponge can find new connections. Thus, in the same way that the physical *pré* is the result of an amalgamation of the remnants of the past physical realms, Ponge's *pré* is the result of a renaissance of past languages and literatures, as well as other arts, such as painting and music. Indeed, the first part of the book is a combination of fragments from different realms and genres out of which the poem proper is born. These preparatory pages, which on the model of Dante's journey take us 'sur les sentiers de la création' (on the paths of creation), are both a journey through a gallery of representational forms as well as a journey into the underground of the poem. In this gallery, from the picture of the 'actual' *pré* at Chantegrenouille to the last illustration, Seurat's *Etude pour un après-midi à la Jatte,* one has passed through photography, painting, music, tapestry, miniature, as well as through history, and across generic boundaries.

I would like to concentrate on two of the illustrations in particular because they present the metaphor of the tapestry that Ponge uses to establish not only the relationship between the 'épaisseur des choses' and the 'épaisseur des mots,' but also to convey the relationship between the textual and the vegetable. The tapestry becomes the medium through which the textile, the textual, and the botanical can merge. The sentence from 'Le Pré' that accompanies the reproduction from a botanical dictionary reads 'milles aiguillées de fil vert font un pré' (FP 131), ['a thousand needles ful of green thread make a *pré*' (MP 146)] using the vocabulary of tapestry. The metaphor thus works in three dimensions: the needle is also a botanical term; a needle of green thread is used as an image for the blade of grass, but also for the acute accents in words. Moreover, the subject of the tapestry plays on modes of representation and reflects the *mise en abyme* of Ponge's poem.

The Persian miniature, on the other hand, presents a whole cosmogony of vegetation, river, birds out of which the text literally seems to soar at the top of the page. Moreover, the Arabic script of the text resembles the notes of music that the birds with their beaks in the air, immediately underneath the text, seem to have just produced. Similarly, in another plate, a musical score, the notes of music resemble blades of grass. Within the poem proper, Ponge compares the *pré* to a Persian carpet: the *pré* is, however, more 'précieux' than the carpet because it is 'tiré à quatre rochers ou à quatre buissons d'aubépine' (FP 83) [stretched neatly from four rocks or four hedges of hawthorn (MP 50)], as one says commonly in French, 'tiré à quatre epingles,' meaning 'dressed up.' The physical thorn of the hawthorn (*aubépine*) recalls the needle of the tapestry or carpet maker, while 'tiré à quatre epingles' points to the way a canvas was held together and the way precious embroidery was ironed in the old days. This Persian miniature sums up the various associations scattered throughout the poem between the drops of rain, the notes of music, the letters on the page, the accents, the birds flying across the *pré* in a direction opposite to the writing (like 'l'accent aigu' on *pré,* like the crossed swords of the duelists, like the crossed needles of the tapestry makers, and of course like the blades of grass). This textile analogue is already present in the title of the book, since one of the meanings of the word 'fabrique' is fabric.

And yet, if vegetation and flowers are commonly associated with the textile, they are even more commonly associated with death and burial. This link is developed in Ponge's *Pré*. As in *The Poet Lying Down* by Chagall, the *pré* in Ponge's poem invites us to lie down; it is our place of rest, soon to become the place of eternal rest, or burial for one of a pair of duelists. This is also Ponge's premature fate, as his poem ends with his typographical burial under the *pré,* out of whose name the fennel and the purslane will grow. It is in this way that one becomes reconciled with nature, returns to the mineral realm, to the 'cendrier universel' which nourishes the *pré* in an endless cycle. This ending indeed takes us back to the title of the book where the initials of Ponge were already inscribed. It is this return which enacts the reconciliation of human beings, nature, poem, and *pré* and ensures their survival.

In *Pour un Malherbe*, Ponge repeats a quotation from Malherbe, which he recognizes as the desire of any writer of any generation: 'Ce que j'écris dure éternellement' [what I write lasts eternally]. In the same text, Ponge writes:

> *A tort ou à raison, j'ai toujours considéré depuis mon enfance, que les seuls textes valables étaient ceux qui pourraient être inscrits dans la pierre; les seuls textes que je puisse dignement signer (ou contresigner), ceux qui pourraient ne pas être signés du tout; ceux qui tiendraient encore comme des objets, placés parmi les objets de la nature: en plein air, au soleil, sous la pluie, dans le vent. C'est exactement le propre des inscriptions. Et certes, je me souvenais, inconsciemment ou non, pensant à cela, des inscriptions romaines de Nîmes, des Epitaphes, etc.* (PM 186)

> *Rightly or wrongly, I have always considered, from the time I was a child, that the only texts that are worthwhile are those that could be inscribed in stone; the only texts that I could agree to sign (or countersign) with any kind of dignity; those that need not be signed at all; those that would still* stand *like objects, placed among the objects of nature: in the open air, in the sun, under the rain, in the wind. This is exactly the nature of inscriptions. And of course, I was recalling, unconsciously or not, while thinking of this, the Roman inscriptions in Nîmes, Epitaphs, etc.*

Following Ponge's explanation of the ending of the poem, and following its narrative thread, some critics have read the death and burial of the poet as the result of the duel between the poet and the object, the outcome of which is the sacrifice of the poet so that the text can be born. As valid as this interpretation might be, the previous quotation from *Pour un Malherbe* offers a different reading which reveals the merging of the *pré* and the epitaph as part of the poet's unconscious. In *Pour un Malherbe*, Ponge associates the (tomb) stones and the blades of grass not only with the name of Malherbe but also with the survival of his own work: 'Quelque chose de mâle (malherbe) de libre (mauvaise herbe) mais quelle herbe? Celle qui croît au pied des remparts ou de belles maisons cubiques bien solides, de ces beaux monuments d'éternelle structure' (PM 12) [Something male (malherbe) something free (weed), but what grass? The kind that grows at the foot of fortified walls or of the beautiful square and solid houses, of those beautiful monuments of eternal structure]. Like Malherbe, whose name Ponge returns to the natural world through translation, Ponge enacts his reincarnation in the vegetable world in *La Fabrique du pré* through the assimilation of the *pré* and his tomb.

Through the ending of the poem, Ponge manages to enact what Derrida, Maurice Blanchot, and Louis Marin tell us every writer wants to do, namely to tell his or her own death, to attend his or her own burial. In *Signéponge*, Derrida points out that the one who signs is already dead, and shows how Ponge's name, related to the object-sponge, is disseminated throughout his work.[18] In *La Fabrique du pré*, Ponge plays on his initials, which he has already encrypted in the title of the book:

> *Voici donc, sur ce pré, l'occasion, comme il faut,*
> *Prématurement, d'en finir.*
>
> *Messieurs les typographes,*
> *Placez donc ici, je vous prie, le trait final.*
>
> *Puis, dessous, sans le moindre interligne, couchez*
> *mon nom,*
> *Pris dans le bas-de-casse, naturellement,*

> *Sauf les initiales, bien sûr,*
> *Puisque ce sont aussi celles*
> *Du Fenouil et de la Prêle*
> <u>*Qui demain croîtront dessus.*</u>
> *Francis Ponge.*

So here, on this pré, is the moment come, as needs be,
Prematurely, to be done with it.

Therefore Gentlemen, typographers,
Place here, I beg you, the final stroke.

Then beneath the line, without the slightest space, couch
my name,
In lowercase, quite naturally,

> *Save for the initials, of course,*
> *Since they are also those*
> *Of Fennel and of Purslane*
> <u>*That tomorrow will grow above.*</u>
> *Francis Ponge.*

(MP 230–31)

Having accomplished the linguistic rebirth of the *pré*, the poet can rest and be buried under the *pré* which becomes his tomb. Rotting under the *pré*, the body of the poet has gone back to the 'cendrier universel,' a mixture of the animal, mineral, and vegetable realm which Ponge's name, as sponge, already connotes. As such, the end of the poem is a symbolic coming back home of the poet. It is a coming back home in the sense that death is always a coming back home of sorts; it is also a coming back home to 'Le monde muet qui est notre seule patrie,' and perhaps just as important, a coming back home to the privileged place of birth and childhood in the South of France where tombstones and grass seem to grow together.

However, the end of the poem is not merely the recounting and enactment of the death and burial of the poet, it is also his rebirth. Indeed, out of the rotting body of the poet, and out of the elements of his name, will ooze the 'Fenouil' (Fennel) and the 'Prêle' (Purslane). The *pré*, as we have already hinted, can never be finished, and can never die. Nor can the consciousness that constructed it and was constructed by it. This is a coming home to the plant world, which in plant lore, has been considered as the habitation of the departed souls, based on the doctrine of the transmigration of souls. The vegetable world is always associated with death and rebirth. Thus, in the 'Le Pré,' the blades of grass are directly connected to the phallus, as well as to the physical tool of writing.

Ponge hopes to write the kind of poetry that can do away with the name. This can be interpreted as Ponge's desire to write about objects in such a way that the reader will no longer need their names in order to recognize them – one way of signing. What I think Ponge wants to achieve is the kind of poetry that will be recognized as his own without the need for his signature outside the text. Then, and then only, will Ponge have signed. In *La Fabrique du pré* Ponge can only sign his name under the bar separating his given name from the poem-become-*pré*, after he has first signed his real and proper name as *Fenouil* and *Prêle*. This real and proper name is the most distinguishing and individualizing part of the name, the *pré-nom* that links the masculine and the feminine, so that we are invited to read the end of the poem not only as a denial or victory over death, but also as a fake death, as the orgasm and life-generating ejaculation resulting from the copulation of the masculine poet with what Ponge calls 'the feminine world.' This is after all what Ponge's poetry is all about: an ejaculation provoking the reader's jubilation: 'L'expression peut être considérée comme une simple éjaculation: donc ne tendant à rien d'autre . . . (une sorte de perfection passive, passive parce qu'on est alors commandé par un souci de dépense purement personnel, purement subjectif dont le but ne nous apparaît pas' (FP 34) [Expression can be considered as a simple ejaculation: and thus having no other purpose ... (a sort of passive perfection, passive because one is then controlled by a purely personal and purely subjective energy, the purpose of which is not apparent)]. If therefore the poet has ejaculated, if the poet is spent, perhaps he can rest and actually sign his real and plural proper name.

Both through its etymology and through its plural combination, the *pré* is both feminine and masculine, both singular and plural. Similarly, Ponge's name has become plural, masculine, and feminine. In *Signéponge,* Derrida sees Ponge's actual signature in his scattering the word *éponge* (sponge) through his discourse. For Derrida, the signature is not necessarily outside the text: to sign one's real name is to sign in the text. In *Glas,* Derrida concentrates on Genet's name, the name of a flower, which unconsciously led him to disseminate flowers all through his discourse. To disseminate fragments of one's name through one's text is a way of signing without necessarily dying, a way also of mastering one's discourse – a game that several writers have played. Before Derrida, Valéry meditated on the survival of poetry and the glory of the poet in these terms: 'La gloire consiste à devenir un thème ou un nom commun, ou une épithète' [Glory consists in becoming a theme or a common noun, or an epithet].[19] In turning his proper name into the names of two herbs, Ponge naturalizes his name, transforms something cultural into something natural, in the same way that he attempted to return the cultural notion of the *pré* to its natural origin.

In *Mille Plateaux,* Deleuze and Guattari point out that one acquires one's name, one's veritable proper name, only when one has opened oneself up to the rhizomatic relationships with the world and with one's unconscious: 'Or le nom ne désigne pas un individu: c'est au contraire quand l'individu s'ouvre aux multiplicités qui le traverse de part en part à l'issue du plus sévère exercice de dépersonalisation qu'il acquiert son nom propre,' that is 'le vrai nom propre, intime prénom qui renvoie aux devenirs, infinitifs, intensités d'un individu dépersonalisé et multiplié' ['The proper name (nom propre) does not designate an individual: it is on the contrary when the individual opens up to the multiplicities pervading him or her, at the outcome of the most severe operation of depersonalization, that he or she acquires his or her true proper name . . . a true proper name, an intimate first name linked to the becomings, infinitives, and intensities of a multiplied and depersonalized individual'].[20] Similarly, in *Pour un Malherbe,* Ponge claims that 'to sign by one's name alone is to banish oneself from the world' (PM 41).

I suggest, therefore, that Ponge, having let himself be constructed by the blades of grass of the *pré* as much as he constructed them through his linguistic re-creation, has gained the privilege of his proper name. The initials of Ponge actually frame the poem as they are encrypted both at the beginning and at the end. Moreover, if read backwards, the poem or the *pré* are both seen as sprouting out of the (dead) body and 'proper' name of the poet. It is of course not by chance that this plural name is also the name of two herbs from his childhood, 'le Fenouil et la Prêle.' If one of them (*la Prêle*) encrypts and reverses the subject and title of his poem, it also happens to designate, as one finds out in Littré, the herb used by workers to polish glass and stone. If Ponge did not know this meaning attached to the purslane, he unconsciously chose the herb that fits the task he assigned himself, to 'refaire le monde' (remake the world) for our pleasure.

CHAPTER FOUR

The Flower, the Fruit, the Feminine

Hélène Cixous

Understand! The first word I ever heard out of any of you was the word 'understand.' Why didn't I 'understand' that I must not play with water – cold, black, beautiful flowing water – because I'd spill it on the palace tiles. Or with earth, because it dirties a little girl's frock. Why didn't I 'understand' that nice children don't eat out of every dish at once, or give everything in their pockets to beggars; or run in the wind so fast that they fall down; or ask for a drink when they're perspiring; or want to go swimming when it's either too early or too late, merely because they happen to feel like swimming. Understand! I don't want to understand. There'll be time enough to understand when I'm old. . . . If I ever am old. But not now.

– Jean Anouilh, Antigone

If it seems impossible to avoid the association between flowers and women, perhaps one should accept it as revealing some truth, the truth of some archaic knowledge, prior to the divisive gaze of modern science. 'Feminist' writer Hélène Cixous, whose name (Cixous, a near anagram of *souci*, the orange marigold) predisposed her, like Genet, to disseminate flowers through her discourse, celebrates in her work the mythical and physical relationship between flowers (and fruit) and women. Accepting the association between women and flowers will of course entail a liberation of woman and flower from the surveillance of the sun, the father, the One, and vision to reintroduce her into the living realm of metamorphoses, multiplicity, the voice, the ear, and the nocturnal – in other words, recognizing her roots. To achieve this, Cixous seems to 'accept' the Hegelian – or simply masculine – association between women and flowers. To revive the apparently trivial nature of male praise, Cixous reinterprets and demonstrates the strength of women and flowers by emphasizing precisely what Hegel attempted to discipline and repress.

In *Speculum de l'autre femme*, Luce Irigaray implicitly associates women and plants in her criticism of phallocentrism as oculocentrism:

> *La* Phusis *est toujours déjà en acte d'appropriation à un telos. Ainsi de la Plante ou même de sa* fleur, *'par exemple.' Encore faut-il qu'un logos ait pu juger de son genre et espèce de plante. Spéculer sur les qualités du végétal? Etc. La sanction de conformité de la plante lui vient d'un autre. D'un être parlant qui plus est philosophiquement. Elle peut être pleine de soi-même en soi-même, mais la décision de cet état sera prononcée par un autre.*

> The physis is *always already being appropriated by a* telos. This is *true of the plant, or even of its* flower, *'for example.' Even so, isn't a* logos *necessary before the genus [and gender] and species of the plant can be determined? Is this speculating on the qualities of the vegetable? Etc. The plant may indeed conform to her own purpose, but another has to certify this. And that other must speak, and speak, moreover, as a philosopher. She may be fully herself in herself, but another has to declare that this is the case.*[1]

Even if what Irigaray says here about flowers applies primordially to women (the subject of her book), a passage from her *Ce Sexe qui n'en est pas un*, even though dealing with women, seems to describe the fate of flowers in the hands of botanists:

Séparer la lumière de la nuit revient à renoncer à la légèreté de notre mélange. A durcir ces hétérogènes qui nous font si continument toute(s). A nous diviser par des cloisons étanches, à nous dissocier en parties, à nous couper en deux, et plus. Alors que nous sommes toujours l'une et l'autre en même temps.

If we divide light from night, we give up the lightness of our mixture, solidify those heterogeneities which make us so consistently whole. We put ourselves into watertight compartments, break ourselves up into parts, cutting ourselves in two, and more, whereas we are always one and the other at the same time.[2]

As these two citations show, both flowers and women are framed by the dominating gaze that sees without seeing, which automatically transforms multiplicity into unity. Like woman, the flower gets her name, gender, and species from another.

Thus, Hegel, in postulating male exertion and will, decrees that woman will be passive, effortless, and allied to chance, that her knowledge is borne by the winds, that to her everything comes easily – *comme une fleur.* Under the name, the flower as flower disappears: women and flowers disappear beneath the denomination 'la femme, la fleur' – the flower has already been pressed under the law of the example, turned into a mere variant of a type. Thus, as Derrida says, 'la fleur est partie' whenever it is folded into the pages of a book or of the law. Like woman, the flower is 'seen' for its name, for its use, and exists for insects or for observers. Under the domination of scientific use, it is subjected (*assujettir* is Rousseau's word to describe the making of a herbarium), labeled, dissected, cut until its living presence has been transformed into a dried specimen, as is the fate of the cyclamen in Freud's 'dream of the botanical monograph' or of any flower in Rousseau's herbaria (see chapter 1).

It is this dominating attitude, dependent on recognition

& categorization, that characterizes Rousseau's 'Lettres sur la botanique,' a series of missives written to teach Madame Delessert and her daughter to 'see' – to see in order to recognize and name flowers. A passage from Rousseau's *Confessions*, also dealing with flowers, points to a more feminine apprehension that allows the flower to exist outside of the confines of vision. As in the case of Freud's botanical monograph, the passage in Rousseau's *Confessions* has to do with the relationship between the flower and the eye. In both cases, however, what is ignored is precisely the object of vision, namely the flower, which does not let itself be ignored, which remains, and even comes back – as flowers tend to do:

En marchant elle [Madame de Warens] vit quelque chose de bleu dans la haye, et me dit: Voilà de la pervenche encore en fleur. Je n'avois jamais vu de la pervenche, je ne me baissai pas pour l'examiner, et j'ai la vue trop courte pour distinguer à terre les plantes de ma hauteur. Je jettai seulement en passant un coup d'oeil sur celle-là, et près de trente ans se sont passés sans que j'aye revu de la pervenche ou que j'y aye fait attention. En 1764 étant à Cressier avec mon ami Du Peyrou, nous montions une petite montagne au dessus de laquelle il a un joli salon qu'il appelle avec raison Belle Vue. Je commençois alors d'herboriser un peu. En montant et regardant parmi les buissons, je pousse un cri de joye: ah voilà de la Pervenche; et c'en étoit en effet. Du Peyrou s'apperçut du transport, mais il en ignoroit la cause; il l'apprendra, je l'espère, lorsqu'un jour il lira ceci. Le lecteur peut juger par l'impression d'un si petit objet, celle que m'ont fait tous ceux qui se rapportent à la même époque.

As we walked, she saw something blue in the hedge, and said to me: 'Look! there are some periwinkle still in flower.' I had never seen any periwinkle, I did not stoop to examine it, and I am too short-sighted to distinguish plants on the ground without doing so. I merely gave it a passing glance, and nearly thirty years elapsed before I saw any periwinkle again, or at least before I noticed any. In 1764 when I was at Cressier with my friend M. Du Peyrou, we were climbing a hill, on the top of which he has built a pretty little look-out which he rightly calls Belle Vue. I was then beginning to botanize a little and, as I climbed and looked among the bushes, I gave a shout of joy: 'Look! there are some periwinkle!', as in fact they were. Du Peyrou noticed my delight, but he did not know its cause; he will learn it, I hope, when one day he reads this. The reader can judge by the effect on me of something so small, the degree to which I have been moved by everything that relates to that stage in my life.[3]

A strange text this: despite its emphasis on 'seeing,' it displays a blindness that allows one to 'see.' Indeed, in this passage about seeing periwinkle, nobody sees 'de la pervenche.' First, Madame de Warens (Rousseau's *Maman*) does not see periwinkle, she sees 'something blue in the hedge' which she calls 'de la pervenche.' And she sees it in passing (*en marchant*), and it is 'de la pervenche encore en fleur,' close to fading, close to being no longer recognizable as 'de la pervenche.' Madame de Warens sees in passing something passing between recognition and nonrecognition. In other words, seeing without seeing, Madame de Warens 'sees' 'de la pervenche.' As for Jean-Jacques, he is at least twice blind: involuntarily ('je n'avais jamais vu de pervenche' and 'j'ai la vue trop courte') and voluntarily ('je ne me baissai pas pour l'examiner'). Laziness and shortsightedness prevent Rousseau from 'seeing,' from consciously allowing into his mind something that somehow gets inscribed there unconsciously.

Thirty years later, a similar scene occurs. This time *Maman* is 'absent' & Rousseau, who has now started studying and collecting flowers (*herboriser*) with his friend M. Du Peyrou, 'recognizes' 'de la pervenche' which he still has never seen before. The whole scene is once again set in terms of seeing. We are at a sight/site, called 'Belle Vue,' where M. Du Peyrou sees Jean-Jacques's *'transport de joie.'*

We might ask first what allows Madame de Warens to recognize 'de la pervenche' without actually 'seeing it' – and this is the equivalent of asking what 'seeing' means. And where does sight come from? And what is it that allows Jean-Jacques to recognize something he had never seen before? It seems that what allows Jean-Jacques to 'recognize' the flower are the words of 'maman' which come back to him and transport him into the past. For it is through a rapport with the past, and with the *fleur qui est partie,* that Rousseau can see what is before his eyes now. This then could lead us to the strange conclusion that the flower speaks first to the ear and only then to the eye, and that it speaks with the voice of the mother. In other words, that there is an invisible and subterranean link – something like a telephone – between the mother and the flower, the past and the present.

If from the side of conventional vision, neither Jean-Jacques nor M. Du Peyrou, nor the *lecteur* can 'understand' what happens, one should perhaps call on the *lectrice* Cixous to explain the mythic telepathic thread between flowers and women, which the masculine eye, when it is able to suspect its existence, always attempts to cut. She seems to 'know' that 'depuis toujours que les fleurs sont des femmes, nous avons toutes vécu une ou deux fleurs' [we have always known that women are flowers, we all have lived one or two flowers].[4] Her knowledge is bound to be different, and to appear strange: it is 'feminine knowledge,' it is the 'archaic knowledge,' knowledge which, according to Derrida, we fear:

Oui, toucher, parfois, je pense que la pensée avant de 'voir' et d'"entendre,' y touche, y met les pattes, ou que voir et entendre revient à toucher à distance – très vieille pensée, mais il faut de l'archaïque pour accéder à l'archaïque. Toucher, donc, des deux bouts à la fois, toucher du côté où la science et la dite objec-

tivité technique s'en emparent maintenant au lieu de lui ré-
sister comme auparavant . . . toucher aussi du côté de nos
appréhensions immédiates, de nos pathies, de nos réceptions,
de nos appréhensions parce ce que nous nous laissons ap-
procher sans rien prendre ni comprendre et parce que nous
avons peur.

Yes, touching, sometimes I think that, before 'seeing' or 'hear-
ing,' thought touches, feels, and that seeing or hearing comes
down to touching at a distance – a very old idea, but one needs
the archaic to reach the archaic. Touching, then, from both
sides at once, from the side of science and so-called technical
objectivity, which seize upon the object rather than resisting it,
as used to be the case . . . touching also from the side of our
immediate apprehensions, of our feelings, our way of receiv-
ing and apprehending things, because we let ourselves be ap-
proached without taking or grasping anything and because we
are afraid.[5]

It is to this archaic, tactile knowledge that Cixous's work returns. This return involves a liberation of a different way of
apprehending, of understanding, which is based on smell-
ing, hearing, and touching, the bodily senses disciplined by
philosophy and psychoanalysis. More important, this liberation involves a recognition of a 'feminine' way of expression. In this case, woman, like the flower, has been silenced
by phallocentrism, excluded from language or poisoned by
it: both are sedentary, passive, immobile, mute – unless we
understand, with Cixous, that they have always expressed
themselves, have always thought, have always known in a
different way, namely through the senses, or more generally
through and with their body. Thus the physical and psychological symptoms of what the male discourse has read
as feminine weakness (intuitiveness, sensitivity, hysteria)
are all advocated in Cixous's work.

To other feminists, especially those who militate for
equal power between man & woman, Cixous's view might

appear as too poetic, too 'romantic,' too idealistic. In fact, those feminists who, either in France or in America, want to '*attack* male institutions' & '*combat* the male culture by direct political action,' have accused Cixous of 'revalorizing traditional feminine stereotypes,' of 'claiming as virtues qualities that men have always found convenient.'[6] Cixous's view of the 'feminine' indeed has nothing to do with a struggle for equal power, with reestablishing an opposition between man and woman, or with the demand that the destructive aspects of masculinity become available to women. For Cixous – as well as for Irigaray, with whom she is often associated – woman always had 'power,' a power of her own, a power of which the repression by male discourse is symptomatic. For both Cixous and Irigaray, women have to be reminded of their power; they must be told who they were (their myth), who they can be again. They need to be heard, allowed to speak their own language, to express their difference, to break the mirror that has always reflected the same, the male, the light, the male law. This is the kind of liberation that Cixous advocates and which needs to precede social transformations.

This is why Cixous can be said to reject 'feminism as a movement too much like men's, a search for power that imitates rather than transcends the phallocentric order.'[7] Besides, for both Cixous and Irigaray, the 'feminine' is not the prerogative of the female, and neither is the masculine the prerogative of the male; it is, despite anatomical determination, a way of apprehending the world, which needs liberation and valorization to the benefit of both men and women. Liberating the 'feminine' in this way is liberating writing and the unconscious. As Cixous points out, 'La poésie n'est que de prendre force de l'inconscient, et que l'inconscient, l'autre contrée sans limite est le lieu où vivent les refoulés: les femmes, ou comme le dirait Hoffmann, les fées' [Poetry is nothing other than accepting the power of the unconscious, and the unconscious, this other limitless place is the place where the repressed live: women, or as Hoffmann would say, the fairies].[8]

To show women what they really are, where they come from, Cixous turns to myth: mainly the myth of Demeter and Persephone which allows her to emphasize the closeness of mother and daughter, as well as woman's closeness to nature – a relationship repressed by phallocentrism. Talking about 'L' ecriture feminine,' Luce Irigaray notes, 'Ce "style" ne privilégie pas le regard, mais rend toute figure à sa naissance, aussi *tactile*. . . . désir du proche, plutôt que du propre' (*Ce Sexe*, 76) ['This "style" does not privilege sight; instead it takes each figure back to its source, which is among other things also *tactile*. . . . desire for the proximate rather than for (the) proper(ty)' (79)]. Cixous's work recounts and advances this old story, this history of woman's transgression of the Law as the law of the proper, of propriety and property. Woman has to touch – especially the flower and the fruit – to discover her own speech, to place her *langue* to the earthen text, the fruit. In *Limonade tout était si infini*, Cixous writes, 'Pourquoi toute l'histoire commençait-elle avec un fruit? Et la chose la plus importante du monde est: oser manger un fruit' [Why did all of history start with a fruit? And the most important thing in the world is: to dare eat a fruit].[9] This primitive scene which repeats itself through history and cultures is not only the biblical or Miltonic story of Eve, but also that of the myth of Persephone and Demeter which Cixous recounts in *Illa*. This scene presents the feminine encounter with the beauty of the world, woman's response to the calling (*l'appel*, but also the apple), of the (mother) earth, which the masculine law always monitors, interrupts, and cuts. Over and over again, one sees this masculine attempt to interrupt this primitive feminine *jouissance*, this proximity to life, which cannot be arrested. In Cixous's rewriting of this primitive scene, the law of man (of the father, of the uncle, of the father of philosophy and of psychoanalysis) can only act as a screen memory temporarily veiling 'la jouissance préhistorique' which 'n'est jamais effacée' (*Limonade*, 28) [the prehistoric ecstasy (which) can never be erased].

The story that repeats itself and gets reread, retold (*ré-citée*) in Cixous's work is the following:

Une personne honnête et simple, sortait d'une forêt de la deux-ième réalité, une personne venant du coeur sauvage de la vie, l'âme toute heureuse à l'idée de découvrir le beau monde aux visages mystérieux. Et à peine faisait quelques pas, se trouvait devant la porte fatale, et tombait comme un panthère humaine dans les filets de la loi. C'était ainsi dans toute les histoires: il y avait de l'invisible' (*Limonade*, 110)

An honest and simple person would come out of a forest of the second reality, a person coming from the wild heart of life, her soul completely elated with the idea of discovering the beauti-ful world with its mysterious faces. And after taking a few steps, she would find herself in front of a fatal door, and would fall like a human panther into the nets of the law. It was like this in all (his)stories, there was something hidden.

We should recognize here not only the story of Eve, but also that of Europa, Alice, Little Red Riding Hood, and others. What all these stories have in common is that they seem to begin with a young girl gathering fruit or flowers. In the story of Eve, as Cixous reinterprets it in *Limonade,* the law of the father (God in this case) is what transforms the call (*appel*) of the apple into an interdiction. By turning an ap-ple into *the* apple, God separated 'les êtres des fruits' [be-ings from fruits]. In this scene, the plural reality of the fruit conceals a worm, the definite article, which transforms the gift into 'un fruit à ne pas' [a fruit not to be picked]: 'C'était donc un fruit. Mais l'épreuve consistait à ne pas le prendre pour un fruit. . . . Et l'histoire dit: ne faites pas attention au fruit. . . . Il suffisait de penser qu'il y avait du Non avant le Oui. . . . Le désir de la loi est de séparer' (*Limonade*, 106, 112) [So it was a fruit. But the test consisted in not taking it for a fruit. . . . And history says: do not pay attention to the fruit. . . . It was sufficient to think that there was No before Yes. . . . The desire of the law is to separate]. This is the law that women will always have to transgress, because their way of thinking implies touching, their way of thinking first says yes. Women, in Cixous's vocabulary are, not 'des êtres humains [human beings],' but 'des êtres à mains [beings with hands],' hands that give and take. The interdiction – literally, the word placed between (woman and the fruit) – which prevents women from reaching out for the gift of the flower, or the fruit, is thus very painful for women:

C'étaient des périodes très douloureuses pour des 'femmes' de leur genre qui avaient besoin de penser comme on respire, avaient besoin de manger des fruits comme on pense, de partager, de tendre une pomme aux lèvres de l'autre, de faire goûter une pensée à l'autre, avaient besoin de penser vivant, de jouir-penser avec des mots frais, de toutes les sortes, de jouir-goûter aux differents sens. Avaient besoin de choisir suivant les jours, les désirs.' (Limonade, 121–22)

Those were very painful times for 'women' of their kind who needed to think as one needs to breathe, had to eat fruit as one needs to think, had to share, to present an apple to the other's lips, to let the other taste a thought, needed to think alive, to enjoy-think with fresh words, of all kinds, to have enjoy-taste the different senses. Needed to choose according to the days, according to the desires.

Playing on the resemblance between the two French words *savoir* (to know) and *savourer* (to savor), and on the mythical stories of knowledge, Cixous defines 'feminine' knowledge as 'Goûter et savoir, goûter est savoir, savoir est goûter, le vrai savoir est un savourer' (*Limonade*, 12) [To taste and to know, to know is to taste, truly knowing is savoring]. As Derrida does in *Glas* and other texts, Cixous seeks out sensual modes of signification other than the occular: the oral, the tactile, the aural zones are all entrusted with speech. Thus, the word 'langue' refers not only to language, but also regains its ordinary meaning of tongue, and, through the Hebrew word *safah,* the sensual meaning of lips. To speak, therefore, first had the physical meaning of touching with the lips, which leads one to imagine a time when speaking was a savoring of words. Feminine language thus has an irreducible 'hysterical' element: it *is* the language of the body. If we add to this the idea that 'connaître' – as Cixous evidently knows – comes from the Greek word *gignosko,* to know first meant discovering, understanding the secrets of the earth (*gi, ge, gè*), but also the secrets of Demeter (*Dè, Gè, Mèter*), the mother earth, the goddess Demeter. In order to know, therefore, one has to take (*prendre et comprendre*) the gifts (the fruit and the flowers) of the earth mother. This is why, when Cixous talks about woman eating fruit, she interprets it as 'on apprend le secret du fruit' [one learns the secret of the fruit]. This is why also there is 'pas de mal' in the fruit, nothing evil, but also nothing masculine (*mâle*) (*Limonade,* 103).

In order to understand this complex relationship between the mother (earth), the daughter, the flower, and the fruit, we turn to *Illa,* a work in which Cixous rewrites the pre-Hellenic myth of Demeter and Persephone-Kore, the mother & the daughter, the earth & its seed. What interests Cixous about the myth of Demeter and Persephone is that it displays the kind of feminine closeness to the earth prior to the fall into the masculine world of vision. This rewriting also allows Cixous to concentrate on the attachment between the mother and the daughter – usually left out of the masculine psychoanalytic and philosophic discourse – and more generally to reestablish the link between human beings and the outside world (of plants, especially) – a link cut at least since Descartes. Against the myth of Oedipus, chosen by Freud, which privileges the father and the son and leads to concepts of separation, struggle, and death, the myth of Demeter and Persephone dramatizes feminine love and *jouissance* and the sensual connectedness of women.

At first, this description of the myth might seem erroneous since in Ovid's *Metamorphoses* and in the Homeric *Hymn to Demeter*, the emphasis seems to be on Demeter's pain at the loss of her daughter Kore. Cixous's reading, however, brings out the impossibility of separating mother and daughter, the earth, the flower, and the fruit, which the myth expresses and celebrates. In the Ovidian account, the myth begins with the primordial scene of innocence, with Proserpina (Kore-Persephone) gathering flowers.

> *Not far from Henna's walls*
> *There is a pool called Pergus, whose deep water*
> *Hears the swans singing, even more than Cayster.*
> *A wood surrounds the pool, and the green leaves*
> *Keep off the sunlight, and the ground is cool,*
> *And the ground is moist, with lovely flowers growing,*
> *And the season is always spring; and in this grove*
> *Proserpina was playing, gathering flowers,*
> *Violets, or white lilies, and so many*
> *The basket would not hold them all, but still*
> *She was so eager – the other girls must never*
> *Beat her at picking blossoms! So, in one moment*
> *Or almost one, she was seen, loved, and taken*
> *In Pluto's rush of love. She called her mother,*
> *Her comrades, but more often for her mother.*
> *Where he had torn the garment from her shoulder,*
> *The loosened flowers fell, and she, poor darling,*
> *In simple innocence, grieved as much for them*
> *As for her other loss.*[10]

This account of the myth emphasizes the atmosphere of innocence associated with feminine friendship and the gathering and abundance of flowers. Cixous stresses this innocence in her version of the myth: the women are in a pastoral setting, sheltered by nature, among friends of their own sex, satisfying their most immediate needs: playing and gathering flowers. It is of course significant that Kore is the one who has gathered the most flowers. As the daughter of Demeter, the mother earth, the giver of flowers and fruit, the one who makes fruit and flowers grow, Kore's gathering of flowers is a simple and innocent response to the gift of the mother. The association between Kore, her comrades and her mother and the flowers is implicit in Kore's grieving for the loss of them all.

In the Homeric *Hymn to Demeter,* the association between the flowers & the nymphs, and especially with Kore, is even more explicit. Moreover, in this version one flower in particular is named as the snare that causes Kore's abduction, defloration, and 'death':

Apart from Demeter, Lady of the golden sword and glorious fruits, she was playing with the deep-bosomed daughters of Oceanus and gathering flowers over a soft meadow, roses, crocuses, and beautiful violets, irises also and hyacinths, and the narcissus, which Earth made to grow at the will of Zeus and to please the Host of Many, to be a snare for the bloom-like girl – a marvelous radiant flower.[11]

In her reading, Cixous isolates the narcissus, and the white lily, which she transforms into an *ancolie* (columbine), a flower associated with the lion (& therefore Zeus) through its common name in French (*herbe de lion*) and with Apollo through its etymology (*aquilegia,* resembling the beak of an eagle). As for the narcissus, the myth records that it is not a gift of Demeter, the mother earth, but rather a flower that she allowed to grow only to please Zeus and his brother Hades. Moreover, through its etymology (Greek, *narke*) and through the myth of Narcissus, the narcissus is associated with self-affection and death, as well as with the exclusion of the other, especially the feminine. Picking the white flower, a symbol of virginity, is therefore to fall under the law of the masculine. This is why Cixous writes in parenthesis: '(Se méfier des fleurs blancs: C'est au moment où une jeune fille cueille un narcisse que la terre casse et l'ioncle rugit)' (*Illa* 14) [Beware of white masculine flowers: It is just when a young woman picks a narcissus that the earth breaks open and the uncle/lion roars]. Cixous plays on the flower as a traditional symbol of virginity.

If in Cixous's work, flowers are ambiguous, it is because of their contradictory cultural associations. Within the myth of Kore and Demeter, the flower is both an image of the gift of woman, a traditional symbol of woman's virginity, and the hymen which binds and separates man from woman. Defloration is what Freud understands any time a woman recounts a dream in which she picks or wants to pick flowers – it is here that the tearing force interrupts feminine *jouissance* and innocent games. Cixous writes,

Et, comme tant d'autres jeunes femmes aux pieds légers [the epithet associated with Persephone in the Hymn to Demeter], *qui n'ont jamais trahi leur mère, elle [Koré] tient en mépris le pouvoir de l'Amour, lui préférant décidément l'amour de l'amour, elle vit parmi ses amies, sans distinction de classe ou de race, jouissant d'une même science de la gaîté, possédant le savoir au-delà des connaissances que des femmes transmettent aux femmes dans les sites verdoyants abrités du soleil symbolique par des couronnes de feuillages, où la nature entière est un voile qui ne provoque pas, ne fait pas l'hymen, dispense la fraîcheur, tient le voyeur écarté, tandis qu'elles satisfont dans les chambres des forêts, aux seins des lacs, sur le giron vert tendre des champs, leurs besoins de bonheur sans limitation de réalité ou d'intensité.* (Illa, 42–43)

And, as many other light-footed women who never betrayed their mothers, she [Kore] despises the power of Love, preferring to it the love of love, she lives among her friends, without any class or race distinctions, enjoying the same science of gaiety, possessing knowledge beyond the knowledge that women transmit to women in green places sheltered from the

symbolic sun, where all of nature is a veil which does not pro-
voke, does not produce a hymen, but provides coolness, keeps
the voyeur away, while they satisfy, in the bedrooms of the
forest, in the midst of lakes (also at the breasts of), on the
tender green lap of the fields, their needs for a happiness with-
out any limitations of reality and intensity.

In this feminine environment, secluded from the blind-
ing light of the sun, from the eye of man, there is no language, no memory, and thus no separation and limitation. Against the restricting love of man (capitalized love:
L'Amour), involved in the binding but separating law of
marriage (*l'hymen*), the feminine love (the love of love,
l'amour de l'amour) is free and unrestrained. Cixous uses
this myth to differ with Freud on femininity. Against Freud,
who claimed that a woman has to detach herself from her
mother – even hate her – and turn to her father as love
object in order to become a woman, Cixous shows the attachment to the mother, here expressed in terms of the relationship between women and maternal nature. Contrary
to Freud who considered the seduction of the daughter by
the father 'unreal,' a mere wish-fulfillment or fantasy on
the part of the daughter, Cixous presents the seduction of
the father/uncle as an interruption of the closeness of the
daughter to her mother & other women. And if this paternal or avuncular seduction is not acted out with passions
and bodies, it will be articulated within the body of the law
which divides mothers and daughters, women and nature.
Generalizing on other cases of 'paternal' seduction, she emphasizes 'toute la série des grotesques apparences sous lesquelles les vieux pervers se sont vus contraints de se pré-
senter dérobés pour enlever les vierges vigilantes' (*Illa*, 71)
[the whole series of grotesque disguises under which the
old perverts have felt compelled to present themselves concealed (also undressed) in order to abduct the vigilant vir-
gins].

However, what is significant about this myth, and about

Cixous's reading of it, is that the seduction of Kore by Pluto, and her disappearance into Hades where she becomes Persephone, does not interrupt the link between her and her mother. The interruption happens and does not happen. This is why Cixous writes, 'La scène qui aurait pu avoir lieu est celle du rapt de la jeune fille dans sa fleur' (*Illa*, 43) [The scene which could have happened is the abduction of the young woman in her prime]. Indeed, the separation happens on the surface, in the world of light and vision, but there is no actual separation since Demeter and Persephone can still communicate at a distance, albeit through another medium – the ear, the voice, the body. Indeed, Demeter apprehends the disappearance of her daughter at a distance, without being there, without seeing her. In the Homeric *Hymn to Demeter*, Demeter addresses herself to Helios and says: 'Through the fruitless air I heard the thrilling cry of my daughter whom I bare, sweet scion of my body and lovely in form, as of one seized violently; though with my eyes I saw nothing.'[12] As this passage suggests, by calling Persephone 'a scion of her body' (the Greek word is *thallos*, a young shoot or twig, and figuratively an offspring), Demeter alludes to a first separation, birth, which did not separate. In *Illa* Cixous presents this (second) disappearance as a screen memory of the separation at birth:

Comment la mère pourrait-elle éviter de se poser, aussi bas que possible, la question: la disparition de la fille s'est-elle faite au moment où elle a cueilli une fleur blanche ou un fleur, ou à un autre moment? Ou bien le moment où elle s'est penchée n'est-il qu'un moment-écran? Une disparition ayant eu lieu auparavant, celle-ci, à laquelle aucune de nous n'était présente, n'étant qu'une deuxième version de la première? Ou la réalisation sur terre, d'une disparition déjà exécutée en une autre topique? (Illa, 79)

How could the mother prevent herself from asking, as low as possible, the question: did the disappearance of the daughter

occur at the moment when she was picking a white flower or a
masculine flower, or at another moment? Or else is the moment
when she bent to pick the flower only a screen? A disappear-
ance having already taken place before, and this one, at which
none of us was present, being only the second version of the
first? Or the realization on earth of a disappearance already
executed in a different topos?

In order to grow as such, in order to exist, the daughter, the flower, needs to detach herself physically from the earth, the mother. To be born is always to detach oneself from the earth, as the Greek *gigomai* (to be born) indicates, but, to know (*gignosko*) is also to recognize the link with the earth, and to rejoice (*gaio*) in its gifts. Moreover, since Demeter is the earth, and Kore the flower, the fruit of the earth, her disappearance from the world above to the underground is also a return to the womb of the earth. Instead of a separation, therefore, her abduction is a return to a kind of prenatal unity, for even male violence is ruled by the larger patterns of separation and renewal. The opening of the earth, which seems to signify death, can also be interpreted as a birth: 'De la fille aucune trace, comme si elle l'avait rêvée, sauf cette absence brûlante dans les entrailles' (*Illa*, 26) [No trace of the daughter, as if she had dreamed her existence, except for this burning absence in her womb]. It is therefore with and within her body that Demeter feels the 'disappearance' of her daughter, with her ears rather than with her eye: 'N'a pas vu sa fille s'éloigner d'elle-même. A entendu un cri rouge foncé presque noir s'éteindre' (*Illa*, 39) [Has not seen her daughter disappear from herself. Has heard a fading dark-red, almost black, scream]. What Demeter hears is something that her ears cannot receive but which her body and mind somehow receive, the stifled cry of Kore.

This silencing of woman, especially of woman's *jouissance*, her splitting in two (the world of light & the world of night) by masculine psychoanalysis, is the point of departure for Irigaray & Cixous's writing. Both show, through myths, that silencing woman is of no avail, since she can always speak from elsewhere. In *Ce Sexe qui n'en n'est pas un*, Irigaray comments on this silencing of woman and on the different language she uses to express herself:

'*Et voilà, Messieurs, pourquoi vos filles sont muettes.' Même si elles jacassent, prolifèrent pithiaquement en mots qui ne signifient que leur aphasie, ou le revers mimétique de votre désir. Et les interpréter là où elles n'exhibent que leur mutisme revient à les soumettre à un langage qui les exile toujours plus loin de ce que peut-être elles vous auraient dit, vous soufflaient déjà. Si seulement vos oreilles n'étaient pas si informées, bouchées de sens, qu'elles sont fermées à ce qui ne fait pas de quelque façon écho au préalablement entendu. En dehors de ce volume déjà circonscrit par la signification articulée dans le discours (du père) rien n'est:* l'afemme. Zone de silence. (*Ce Sexe*, 111)*

'And this, gentlemen, is why your daughters are mute.' Even if they chatter, proliferate pythically in words which only signify their aphasia, or the mimetic underside of your desire. And interpreting them where they exhibit only their muteness means subjecting them by a language that exiles them at an ever increasing distance from what perhaps they would have said to you, were already whispering to you. If only your ears were not so well informed, clogged with meaning(s), that they are closed to what does not in some way echo the already heard. Outside of this volume already circumscribed by the signification articulated in (the father's) discourse, nothing is: awoman. Zone of silence. (113)*

It is because woman is always at least double, always here and there, because she represents the other side of masculine discourse and *jouissance,* that woman has to be reduced to silence. Her language speaks of the earth, of love, of the mother, a language for which the father/uncle has no ear. Her punishment, whether she is called Antigone or Persephone, will always be a silencing through entombment.

Comment elle [Antigone] rend manifeste, en s'affrontant au discours qui fait loi, cet étayage souterrain qu'elle garde, cette autre 'face' du discours qui fait crise quand elle apparaît au grand jour. D'où son renvoi dans la mort, son 'enterrement' dans l'oubli, le refoulement – la censure? – des valeurs qu'elle représente pour la Cité: rapport au 'divin,' à l'inconscient, au sang rouge.' (Ce Sexe, 162)

How by confronting the discourse that lays down the law, she makes manifest that subterranean supporting structure that she is preserving, that other 'face' of the discourse that causes a crisis when it appears in broad daylight. Hence her being sent off to death, her 'burial' in oblivion, the repression – censure? – of the values that she represents for the City-State: the relation to the 'divine,' to the unconscious, to the red blood. (167)

As we have already seen, entombment does not silence Antigone. Like Persephone, her voice is heard: like the unconscious, the flower cannot be cut off; it reappears disguised. The relationship between Antigone and the 'red blood' mentioned by Irigaray is also present in the myth of Persephone. In this myth, the color of the blood is the color of the stifled cry of Persephone's defloration which Demeter hears. It is also the color of the pomegranate, the poisoned gift of Pluto, which ensures her return to him. Yet the blood-colored fruit is also what ensures her survival and return to her mother and the world of light.

What Cixous's reading emphasizes is this other side of discourse, the feminine discourse which speaks to the ear, which spins a thread between mother & daughter, the seed & the earth, woman & flower. Playing on the name of Kore, Cixous calls upon another silenced daughter, Cordelia – from Shakespeare, but also from Kierkegaard. Among all the wordplay on Kore's name, the most significant is 'corde il y a' (there is a thread). Cixous also calls her 'corps de il y a.' Returning to German, the language of the mother and to the Heideggerian *es gibt* – a translation of 'il y a,' Cixous transforms woman into the body of the giver. Demeter is celebrated as the giver of fruit and flowers. Hers is the free gift which does not become a debt – as opposed to the gift of the father, which establishes property. It is significant that Demeter, while looking for her daughter incognito, says that her name is *Doso*, that is, 'I will give.' There is therefore no end to the giving of the mother; and it is because of the infinity of the gift that Persephone never dies. As in the world of vegetation, Persephone-Kore has to be sown in the ground in order to reappear in the spring.

In the usual interpretation of this vegetation myth, Demeter and Persephone-Kore are in fact one and the same person, and together with Hecate, they represent the triadic goddess of vegetation: Kore, the seed or green corn; Demeter, the ripe corn; and Hecate, the harvested corn. 'La première Première et sa fille la deuxième et troisième, parfois appelées Déméter et Perséphone, souvent simplement appelées "les Déesses" ou les pommes' (*Illa*, 203) [The first First and her daughter the second and third, sometimes called Demeter and Persephone, often simply called the 'Goddesses' or the apples].

Whenever Cixous wants to recall the communication at a distance between Demeter and Persephone, the image that crops up is that of the telephone, which literally means the distant voice, as well as the communication between the voice and the ear that characterizes feminine communication. The telephone, as an image of the thread, the cord, between mother and daughter, between earth and seed, transforms the absence into presence, reestablishes proximity beyond time and space.[13] The thread, as of the telephone, is what allows Demeter to know that Persephone has disappeared – it is as if Persephone were telephoning Demeter. Moreover, there is a central switchboard of women with fine hearing who transmit the call:

Entre celle qui a perdu sa réponse et celle qui reste inaudible, des triples femmes aux longues oreilles pour recueillir le cri au

bord du silence, le sauver de la noyade, une aréthuse ou une
autre hécate, pour transmettre à la mère l'appel de la fille, ou
une angela, ou une des nombreuses nymphes adoptives qui se
relayent pour rétablir les communications quand la femme a
été coupée de la mère par un coup d'oncle; et entre les séparées,
mille amies pour réparer l'absence, une chaîne de femmes pour
faire passer la présence par dessus le passé. (Illa, 82–83)

Between the one who has lost her answer and the one who
remains inaudible, there are triple women with long ears to
collect the cry from the threshold of silence, to save it from
drowning. An arethusa or another hecate to transfer to the
mother the call of the daughter, or an angela, or one of the
numerous adoptive nymphs who relay to reestablish the com-
munication when a woman has been cut off from the mother by
an uncle stroke; and between the ones who are separated, there
are a thousand friends to repair the absence, a chain of women
to allow presence to override the past.

The chain of women here resembles a daisy chain; a children's game called 'téléphonie arabe,' whereby a word is
passed on from mouth to ear; a switchboard; but also the
writing of a multiple-voiced text, what Cixous will call
'feminine writing': 'Writing in the feminine is passing on
what is cut out by the Symbolic, the voice of the mother . . .
the most archaic force that touches the body is one that
enters by the ear and reaches the most intimate point.'[14]

It is significant that, whenever Persephone is mentioned
in a discourse, her name is inevitably linked with communication at a distance, especially between the dead and the
living, the past and the present. Thus, under the title 'Perséphone,' Michel Leiris invokes the goddess to enable him
to retrieve his childhood memories:

De ces expériences qu'aucune crasse n'a ternies – le temps se
bornant à les revêtir d'une patine légère, qui ne fait qu'adoucir
un peu leurs contours et en parachever la fusion dans une
commune 'atmosphère' – quelques unes plus engagées peut-

être que les autres dans l'épaisseur touffue de la nature, m'ont paru, de ce fait pouvoir être rassemblées en une même rubrique. Et j'ai choisi pour le signe sur lequel les placer, le nom tout-à-fait floral et souterrain de Perséphone, arraché ainsi à des noirceurs terrestres et haussé jusqu'au ciel en tête de chapitre.

Out of those experiences which no dirt has tarnished – time having contented itself with covering them with a light patina, which only softens their outlines and accomplishes their fusion in a common 'atmosphere' – it seemed to me that some, perhaps more involved than others in the bushy thickness of nature, could therefore be gathered under a single rubric. And I chose as a sign under which to classify them the completely floral and underground name of Persephone, torn out of its earthly darkness and elevated to the sky as chapter heading.

In this view of the act of writing, memories are supposed to sprout like Persephone, like the flower. When playing on the name of Persephone, Leiris finds significance in the first part of her name which he reads homonymically as the French *percer,* to pierce. Piercing the ground (like the flower in the spring, especially if its name is *perce-neige*), piercing voice (*Perse + Phone,* like the cry of Persephone at the moment of her abduction), piercing the ear (of Demeter, who heard her daughter's disappearance) are recurrent motifs in Leiris's essay.[15] They are meant to emphasize the growth of writing out of the dark recesses of the unconscious, following the fate of Persephone.

Significantly, the first memory brought up by the name of Persephone is that of the gramophone of childhood, which the young Leiris used to call 'graphophone.' It is of course not by chance that the gramophone resembles a flower, and a gigantic ear, and that its name resembles that of Persephone. Leiris describes the old gramophone to make the reader see how the music seems to emerge from a dark underground via a penetrating needle or jewel in the flower-shaped ear of the speaker. Metaphors of speaking and hearing, piercing and blooming, darkness and light are combined in the gramophone. In Leiris's essay, the words of the song, the memories, the flowers appear then as an emanation of the music of the earth. As in Rilke's *Sonette an Orpheus,* the gramophone, the flower, becomes the ear of the earth out of which past memories emerge. In Leiris's writing, the ear is also the site of linguistic metamorphoses, out of which is born the signification of the past. What unfolds out of the ear also resembles the floral birth of the work of art in Proust. Indeed, for Leiris, writing is a response to the silenced voice which pierces your ears and makes words grow:

Perséphone, puits artésien planté dans l'épaisseur de la nature et révélant les secrets souterrains sous les espèces d'un jet roucoulant et suraigu, serais-tu vraiment ce jaillissement, O Perséphone, ou ne le deviendras-tu, qu'au hasard d'une métaphore?

Persephone, artesian well planted in the thickness of nature and gathering the underground secrets under the species of a cooing and piercing stream, could you, O Persephone, be this springing up, or would you only become so in a chance metaphor?[16]

In Cixous's work, as in Leiris's, the telephone, the link between past and present, above and below, is like 'telepathy,' a voice that 'touches' at a distance.

In 'Dreams and Occultism,' Freud compares the relationship between two unconsciouses to the telephone and wireless telegraphy, but he rejects this kind of communication at a distance as improbable because he cannot accept the idea of unmediated communication. Discussing Freud's rejection of telepathy, Derrida writes,

La vérité, ce à quoi j'ai toujours du mal à me faire: que la non-télépathie soit possible. Toujours difficile d'imaginer qu'on

puisse penser quelque chose à part soi, dans son for intérieur,
sans être surpris par l'autre. . . . Difficile d'imaginer une thé-
orie de ce qu'ils appellent encore l'inconscient sans une théorie
de la télépathie.'

In truth, something I always have difficulty getting used to is
that nontelepathy might be possible. It is always difficult to
imagine that one could think something for oneself, within
oneself, without being surprised by the other.[17]

Similarly in 'Tympan,' *Ulysse gramophone,* and *La Carte pos-*
tale, Derrida uses the image and technology of the gramophone and telephone to show the impossibility of exclud-
ing the other from the discourse of the self. To prove that
what has come to be called 'the interior monologue' is a
misnomer, Derrida calls Leopold Bloom in Joyce's *Ulysses*
'the man-at-the-telephone.' In this respect all speaking and
all writing is always a conversation with the other. One
could even say that writing essentially takes place on the
model of the relationship between Persephone and Demeter, on the model of the telephone call. Hence Derrida's re-
frain, 'In the beginning was the telephone,' is opposed to
the logocentric credo 'in the beginning was the word.'[18]

Derrida could be writing about Persephone, and about
the flower, when he says of Bloom that 'son être là est
un être-au-téléphone. . . . Un *Dasein* qui n'accède à lui-
même que depuis l'Appel (*Ruf*), un appel venu de loin, qui
ne passe pas nécessairement par des mots et qui d'une cer-
taine manière ne dit rien' [his being there is a being on the
phone. . . . A *Dasein* (Being) which only comes to itself from
the Call (*Ruf*), a call from far, and which does not necessarily pass through words, and which in a certain way does
not say anything].[19] For it is through the 'womanly man,'
Bloom, that Joyce allows Ulysses to speak. Bloom is the
flower whose roots are open both to the Greek and Jewish
calls from Homer and Zion. And it is to him, as to life, that
Molly, the flower of the mountains, will always say Yes. The

telephonic model which Derrida analyzes in *Ulysse gramophone* is that of the French phone call, which is always a call for the yes, namely the 'allo, oui' which opens the response of the person at the other end, the yes to language, the affirmation before speech which any conversation presupposes.

This yes of the mother to the daughter's call, of the daughter to the mother's gift, this gift passed on between women becomes associated in Cixous's texts with feminine writing as well as with feminine *jouissance*. In *Ulysse gramophone,* Derrida addresses Cixous on the question of 'la jouissance par l'oreille' [pleasure through the ear] and her suggestion that 'jouir par l'oreille soit plutôt féminin' [pleasure through the ear would rather be feminine]. His affirmative answer reads: 'Le oui serait alors de la femme . . . de la mère, de la chair, de la terre' [The yes would belong to women . . . to the mother, to the flesh, to the earth]. The 'oui,' the 'viens' (come), the 'reste' (remain[s]) is always said of or to the mother in Derrida's feminine texts. As he states in *Glas,* describing what he calls the law of 'obséquence' (*obsèque* [burial] + *conséquence*), the mother, as natural process, is always the one who remains, who attends your burial, & who dictates and countersigns what you write.[20] It is the voice of the mother, a voice from a distance, a voice from close by, a voice from the interior that Cixous describes: 'Un appel venu de l'étranger. L'écriture. Personne écrit. Personne appelle. L'écriture a téléphoné. Une voix de très loin, de très près. Viens me chercher. Je me perds de plus que près, de l'intérieur' (*Illa,* 57) [A call from abroad. Writing. Nobody/Somebody writes. Writing called. A voice from far, from close by. Come and find me. I am losing myself from close by, from the inside]. Cixous's feminine writing is a quest for the voice of the absent mother, for the gifts of the mother, the flowers that the mother earth allows to grow for our *jouissance*.

Cixous is also always on the telephone – at either end,

sometimes calling, sometimes being called. In *Limonade*, she calls Elli, 'her daughter,' to tell her that she has written a letter to her. The telephone call, which reestablishes the proximity of mother and daughter, assures her that the letter she sends has already arrived at its destination, that the gift has not become a law but has been given freely and received with the same generosity it was given. More important for us, Cixous receives phone calls from things, especially from flowers and fruit – which, as we have argued, are always already women:

Ce qui n'empêchait pas la beauté de lui apparaître, la chose de s'adresser à elle, aussi audiblement que si elle lui téléphonait: tu m'entends? elle-même repondait: oui, je t'entends. (Limonade, 191)

This did not prevent beauty from appearing to her, the thing from addressing her, as audibly as if she were calling them: do you hear me? She herself would answer: yes, I hear you.

Calling the flower, calling the daughter is eventually the same event. In *With ou l'art de l'innocence*, Cixous comments on her attraction to the metaphor of the telephone: 'Téléphoner ne veut pas dire parler de loin au contraire c'est parler jusqu'au fond du très très près, d'un intérieur à l'autre, à voix réellement désarmées, d'une innocence à l'autre, sans médiation' [To telephone does not mean to speak from a distance; on the contrary, it is to speak from the very depth of closeness, from one inside to the other, with utterly disarmed voices, from one innocence to the other, without mediation].[21] In this context, the telephone is what establishes a relationship between two unconsciouses, a telepathic link that allows one to be *with* the other, or even to recognize the other in oneself. For, as Cixous and Irigaray know, woman, like the flower, is never one, she is the one *and* the other, always here *and* elsewhere. Her plural nature can only be written – as the *gl* of *Glas,* and the *or* of Rilke – in the key of *et,* of 'and,' the endless and free agglutinations of elements. This is the feminine syntax of Joyce's Molly Bloom and Anna Livia Plurabelle, a syntax based on juxtaposition as opposed to the masculine syntax of subordination. The key of *et* allows woman to be both one and the other, both here and there; it allows Cixous to inscribe within her discourse her own plural nature as francophone.

If one seems to forget that the 'French writer' Hélène Cixous was born in Oran, Algeria, she never forgets; she even writes in order not to forget. *Et* links Paris and Oran, France and Algeria, the capital and its colony. Oran thus figures in her work as a psychological, social, and political elsewhere, the origin of a conscious and unconscious writing. At the personal level, Cixous's heritage (her father a Sephardic Jew of Spanish, Moroccan, Algerian descent; her mother an Ashkenazic Jewess of Austrian, Czechoslovakian, Hungarian, and German origins) puts her in a position of exile from the mother tongue. As in the case of Joyce, this lack of a mother tongue causes an obsession with language. Thus in 'De le scène de l'inconscient à la scène de l'Histoire: chemin d'une écriture,' Cixous remarks,

A elle [sa mère] je dois de n'avoir jamais eu avec aucune langue un rapport de maîtrise, de propriété; d'avoir toujours été en faute, d'avoir toujours voulu m'approcher délicatement de la langue, jamais mienne, pour la lècher, la humer, adorer ses différences, respecter ses dons, ses talents, ses mouvements. Surtout la garder en l'ailleurs qui la porte, laisser intacte son étrangeté, ne pas la ramener ici, pas la livrer à la violence aveugle de la traduction. Si tu ne possèdes pas une langue, tu peux être possédé par elle: Fais que ta langue te reste toujours étrangère. Aime la comme ta prochaine.

I owe to her [her mother] never having had any relationship of mastery, of property, with any language; to have always been at fault, to have always wanted to approach any language – never mine – delicately, to lick it, to smell it, to worship its differences, to respect its gifts, its talents, its movements. More

144

than anything, to keep it in the elsewhere which carries it, to leave intact all its strangeness, not to bring it back here, not to deliver it to the blind violence of translation. If you do not possess a language, you can be possessed by it: Let your language remain a stranger to yourself. Love it like your (female) neighbor.[22]

Thus, for Cixous, language is a gift, but never a given. It never is an object or the material of writing; it is rather that which one has to approach delicately so that it gives itself freely. Hence, the abundance of puns in Cixous's writing, puns that are never a gratuitous game, but rather the sign of the acceptance of language as something alive, as a dynamic principle that signifies beyond the mastery and dominion of the writer. Language, in Cixous's work, resembles the language of dreams. It is the feminine language linked to the unconscious where associations happen freely and without repression. It is the language of the Yes, of the *et,* removed from the name and no of the father.

Indeed, in *Le Portrait du soleil,* Cixous disseminates the word 'Oran' to see what associations will emerge, and to allow her place of birth to reappear. To make the portrait of the sun is, of course, an act of defiance, since the sun is the figure of the father. To transform the sun into an orange is to move from the masculine to the feminine, from the father to the mother, from the one to the many, from the law to the gift – and to return to Oran.

The link between Oran, the sun, and the orange is quite natural. The orange is the shape of the sun, it is also the color of the sun rising and setting. The orange is also a fruit from Oran, a fruit which comes from another country and another language: *naranga* in Arabic. If the orange comes to represent woman or pregnant woman, it is not simply because of its form, but because this fruit is plural and bears in itself the seed of the life of the other. And this is not just any orange, it is the homonymic result of the agglutination of two semes: 'Oran' and 'je,' which functions as the actual signature of Cixous, a signature in which the 'I' of the writer inscribes itself as an appendix to her native city.

In 'Chemin d'une écriture,' Cixous explains this discovery:

Un de mes premiers trésors fut le nom de ma ville natale: Oran. . . . Par Oran, je suis entrée dans le secret de la langue. J'ai découvert que ma ville faisait fruit par la simple addition de moi: Oran-je – Orange. J'ai découvert que le mot avait le mystère du fruit.

One of my first treasures was the name of my native city: Oran. . . . Through Oran I penetrated the secret of language. I discovered that my city became a fruit if I only added myself to it: Oran-je – Orange. I discovered that the word possessed the fruit's secret.[23]

And in *Le Portrait du soleil,* she writes, 'L'orange est mon fruit de naissance et ma fleur prophétique. La première fois que j'ai coupé un mot, c'était elle. Je l'ai coupé en deux morceaux inégaux: un plus long et un plus court [Oran-je]' [The orange is my birth-fruit and my prophetic flower. The first time I cut a word, it was that one. I cut it in two unequal parts: one longer and one shorter].[24] One notices here the transformation of the masculine into the feminine in the passage from 'le fruit' to 'elle,' as well as the relationship between the word and the fruit. There is a secret in the fruit as in the word. To discover the secret of the fruit and of the word, one has to savor it, put one's *langue* to it. And as one can cut a fruit, one can cut a word. But to dare to eat the fruit, to dare to cut the word, are both transgressions of the masculine law of unity and identity.

Oran resonates in Cixous's work where it functions as an internal signature, as something inseparable from her writing. In general, one notices a real attraction to the syllables or phonemes *or, a, ora,* as well as for the colors yellow and orange, the golden color of the sun, of the orange, of some flowers, and of their pollen. I suggest that, in addition to the conscious key of *et*, Cixous is writing, like Rilke, in the unconscious key of *or*. Through this key, Cixous signs her work, returns to her origin in Oran, as well as to a vegetable origin which she attributes to women. Thus in *Illa*, commenting on her birth as writer in 'le jardin d'essai' – a real garden in Algiers – Cixous plays with the word 'fruit' which she uses as a verb to refer to herself and to her writing: 'j'ai frui,' which she calls a 'prime-verbe.' A passage follows in which the word *Oran* is split and disseminated into its various phonemes:

'*Frui*' *est l'inouï d'une fleur, le souffle de son éclosion. Frui est le bruit que fait un bouton d'or s'exhaussant vers la lumière. A l'école des herbes spontanées j'ai appris des boutons d'or, à laisser les choses se livrer fidèlement à leur propre épanouissement. . . . Frui est le cri d'or que pousse une grenouillette au soleil. Des midis j'ai frui d'un concert d'or et de bois. Les boutons d'or sont des sourires. Coupés de leur source ils perdent toute nécessité d'être et s'éteignent. On ne peut les séparer du visage de l'origine. Au jardin j'ai su le secret: il y a des fleurs dont les pétales sont des lamelles de lumière émise de manière maternelle par la terre. Des écailles de lumière originale. Et l'orange flux de la terre quand par inspirations elle s'associe l'odeur du pressant humide de l'air tout contre elle, donne forme aux soucis. Les soucis sont donc composés aussi: une noisette de l'odeur consistante de l'air en présence, contenue réchauffée, dans un seau plein de morceaux de couleur pure orange sans mélange. Les soucis sont des fleurs entièrement naturelles. Le souci comme oeuvre de l'orange – L'orange comme puissance et origine du souci.* (Illa, 140–41)

'*Frui*' *is the inaudible of a flower, the breath of its blossoming. Frui is the noise that a buttercup makes while rising to the light. At the school of spontaneous herbs, I learned from the buttercups to let things deliver themselves freely to their blossoming. . . . Frui! is the cry of a little frog in the sun. Some* noons, I 'fruied' from a golden and wooden concert. Buttercups are smiles. Cut from their source, they lose all reason for being and they fade out. One cannot separate them from the face of the origin. In the garden, I found out the secret: there are flowers whose petals are strips of light given out in a maternal way by the earth. Scales of original light. And the orange, flux out of the earth when, inspirationally, it associates itself with the pressing humidity of the air, gives shape to marigolds. Marigolds are thus also composites: a knob of the consistent smell of the air present, contained reheated, in a pail full of segments of pure orange color without any mixing. Marigolds are purely natural flowers. The marigold as the work of the orange – the orange as work of the marigold.

I do not know whether there are buttercups (*boutons d'or*) or marigolds (*soucis*) in Oran – marigolds that Cixous says 'poussent au bord de la mer' [grow along the sea]. And it hardly matters. What is significant here is the dissemination of the fragments of Oran, the colors and flowers associated with it, especially the movement from the buttercup, to the sun, to the marigold.

Cixous also finds this phoneme *or*, which is strewn throughout her writing, & which brings her back to Oran, in Clarice Lispector's name, which begins with the name of another flower, the lily (*lis*). The inspiration which Clarice Lispector is for Cixous is brought about by pollination, fertilization at a distance:

Elle [Clarice Lispector] souffle sur mon être un vent chargé de pollens. J'en ai partout. Elle a de sa poussière sur tout le corps, sur les paupières, sur les cils, sur les lèvres je sens sa sèche finesse d'or sous mes dents, elle lèche et j'avale sa poussière incroyablement fine, elle lit tout à travers son vent jaune paille sans saveur, elle voit tout à travers le mouvement provocant de ses nuées de pensées en haute tempête, je suis à la trace de la grande Clarice à pas d'or, elle écrit à sa clarté de grande nuit lunaire résonnante des ténors de ses étoiles. (Illa, 185)

*She blows on my being a pollen-filled wind. I have it every-
where. She has dust on her whole body, on her eyelids, on her
eyelashes, on her lips I feel her dry golden thinness in my
teeth, she licks and I swallow her incredibly thin dust, she
reads everything through her tasteless yellow wind, she sees
everything through the provocative movement of her clouds of
thoughts in a high storm, I follow the trace of the great Clarice
with golden thread, she writes by the light of a big lunar night
resounding with the tenors of her stars.*

Feminine writing happens in a world of flowers where
schenken is *schicken:* to give is to send, and the gift is *l'envoi.*
What Cixous and Lispector share, then, is, as their names
indicate, the yellow fertilizing dust which they both disseminate freely. Thus Cixous is willing even to accept the
gift of Hegelian classification, which was applied with the
force of a lawgiver – or a botanist: women are like plants,
breathing in ideas. It is useless to consider why Hegel, the
imperial voice of the law, must plead ignorance about the
modes of woman's education ('Who knows how?' Hegel
wonders). Cixous's works are an answer to this question.

Conclusion

*Are departed those who believed that the flower signified, sym-
bolized, metaphorized, metonimized . . . –* Derrida, *Glas*

Few concepts are more suspect in current thinking
than 'nature' and the 'natural.' And yet in some re-
spects it is precisely such concepts that I have attempted to rehabilitate – through reinterpretation – in this
book. I have done so by concentrating on the most 'innocent,' the most inoffensive (some might say the most sentimental) of natural expressions: the flower. But what we
have seen in the preceding essays, drawing on Freud and
Proust, Pelt and Derrida, is how evasive, multivalent, and
abundant this natural innocence really is: how this most
familiar emblem of the 'poetic' is indistinguishable from a
constant dedication to stratagems and conceals within it
what Proust has called 'a whole unconscious element of
literary production.' So perhaps we need to consider nature
'itself' as a less suspicious concept than the structuralist
thinking – so much encouraged by Lévi-Strauss's celebrated opposition of the raw and the cooked – which opposes this concept to something called 'culture.' So much is
evident in Pelt's provocative subtitle: *Amours et civilisations
végétales.*

Nature, the natural, organicism: such terms can no
longer – forty years after Watson and Crick discovered the
structure of DNA – serve as mere synonyms for unexamined
'metaphysical' principles preceding the formative and ideo-

logical work of culture. In the stratagems of flowers one finds not only a model for the workings of the unconscious and language, one discovers a kind of precedent – a first draft, as it were. The 'unconscious' which one sees at work in the realms of nature and culture, plants and people, is not only the psychological reserve which Freud and his followers cultivate. It signifies a wider and less confined reserve of actions and behavior alien to explicit intentionality and motivation and shared by organisms and minds, flowers & literary texts. So when Derrida produces in *Glas* a cross-fertilization of philosophy and literature, Hegel and Genet, we should recognize his work not only as critical and aesthetic, but as biological – which is to say, as an attempt to situate the literary mind in a broader context than the one provided by the conventions of psychobiography. So too when Proust announces that he felt that he had discovered the 'whole unconscious element of literary production,' Proust is writing as a botanist, a psychologist, and an artist. And it is according to these principles that I have tried to read him and the other writers in this book.

Notes

INTRODUCTION

1. On this topic, see Jack Goody, 'The Secret Language of Flowers.' *Yale Journal of Criticism* 3 (1990): 133–52. See also Alan Bewell, 'Keat's "Realm of Flora,"' *Studies in Romanticism* 31 (Spring 1992): 71–98.

CHAPTER 1

1. Georges Bataille, 'Le Langage des fleurs,' *Oeuvres complètes,* 12 vols. (Paris: Gallimard, 1970), 1:173. When not otherwise specified, translations are mine. Generally, I have modified published translations whenever I saw fit.

2. The origins of most flowers' names are complex matters for botanists. In the case of the narcissus, some maintain that its name derives from the Greek *narke,* meaning 'torpor,' which suits the narcotic properties of the flower, while others prefer the mythic origin.

3. Jacques Derrida, *Glas* (Paris: Galilée, 1974), 21b; Derrida, *Glas,* trans. John P. Leavey, Jr., and Richard Rand (Lincoln: Nebraska UP, 1986), 15b. Hereafter these references, abbreviated GL (with their respective page numbers) are given in the text.

4. G. W. F. Hegel, 'Phänomenologie des Geistes' in *Werke* 3 (Frankfurt: Suhrkamp Verlag, 1970), 507; Hegel, *The Phenomenology of Spirit,* trans. A. V. Miller (Oxford: Oxford UP, 1979), 420.

5. G. W. F. Hegel, 'Grundlinien der Philosophie des Rechts' in *Werke* 7 (Frankfurt: Suhrkamp Verlag, 1970), 319–20; Hegel, *The Philosophy of Right,* trans. T. M. Knox (Oxford: Oxford UP, 1978), 263–64.

6. For a complete discussion of the role of Antigone in Hegel, see GL 160a–187a; 141a–197a.

7. Cited in Lesley Gordon, *Green Magic: Flowers, Plants, and Herbs in Lore and Legend* (New York: Vintage, 1977), 23–24.

8. Marie Bonaparte, 'De la mort et des fleurs,' *Revue française de psychanalyse* 1 (1987): 234.

9. Sigmund Freud, 'Die Traumdeutung,' *Gesammelte Werke* 8 (London: Imago, 1942), 175. Freud, *The Interpretation of Dreams,* trans. James Strachey (New York: Avon, 1965), 202. Further page references to these works appear in parentheses in the text.

10. I have borrowed the term *verbarium* (*verbier*) from Nicolas Abraham and Maria Torok's *Cryptonymie: Le Verbier de l'homme aux loups* (Paris: Aubier Flammarion, 1976). Even though Abraham and Torok never say where the word *verbier* comes from, it seems obvious that they coined it on the model of the word *herbier* (*herbarium*). My return of the word to its 'origin' implies the relationship between the verbarium and the herbarium but also intimates that there is a relationship between Abraham and Torok's anasemic reading and the botanical model of dissemination that I discuss here.

11. Hugh Macmillan, *The Poetry of Plants* (London: Pitman, 1907), 13.

12. M. Grieve, *A Modern Herbal* (New York: Hafner, 1971), 125.

13. Claude Lévi-Strauss, *The Savage Mind* (Chicago: U of Chicago P, 1968), 191, 216.

14. Jean-Marie Pelt, *Les Plantes: Amours et civilisations végétales* (Paris: Marabout, 1980–81), 151, 174. My translation.

15. I am referring to Rousseau's 'Huit Lettres élémentaires sur la botanique à Madame Delessert,' published as *Le Botaniste sans maître ou: Manière d'apprendre seul la botanique* (Paris: Métaille, 1983); Goethe's 'Die Metamorphose der Pflanzen,' *Werke,* 5th ed. (Hamburg: Christian Wegner Verlag, 1966), 13:64–101; Goethe's *Botanical Writings,* trans. Bertha Müller (Honolulu: U of Hawaii P, 1952); and Ruskin's 'Proserpina,' *Complete Works,* vol.25, ed. E. T. Cook and Alexander Wedderburn (London: Allen, 1906).

16. In *Green Magic,* Lesley Gordon introduces his discussion of 'the doctrine of signatures' as follows: 'Many of the ancient herbalists believed that a number of plants had been stamped by God with the image of their properties, that those who gathered them might read' (27).

17. Pelt, *Les Plantes,* 245.

18. Marcel Proust, *A la recherche du temps perdu,* 3 vols. (Paris: Gallimard, 1954), 2:603; Proust, *Remembrance of Things Past,* 3 vols., trans. C. K. Scott-Moncrief and T. Kilmartin (New York: Vintage, 1982), 2:625.

CHAPTER 2

1. Jacques Derrida, 'La Mythologie blanche: La métaphore dans le texte philosophique,' *Marges de la philosophie* (Paris: Minuit, 1972), 324; Derrida, *Margins of Philosophy,* trans. Alan Bass (Chicago: U of Chicago P, 1982), 271.

2. Rousseau, *Le Botaniste sans maître ou: Manière d'apprendre seul la botanique* (Paris: Métaille, 1983), 112.

3. John Ruskin, 'Proserpina,' *Complete Works* (30 vols.), vol.25, ed. E. T. Cook and Alexander Wedderburn (London: Allen, 1906), 249–50. Further references are in parentheses in the text.

4. Charles Darwin, *The Origin of Species* (New York: New American Library, 1958), 185.

5. Michel Foucault, *Les Mots et les choses* (Paris: Gallimard, 1966), 146; Foucault, *The Order of Things* (New York: Random House, 1973), 134.

6. Georges Poulet, *L'Espace proustien* (Paris: Gallimard, 1963), pp.19–23.

7. See Philip Kuberski, 'Proust's Brain,' in his *Persistence of Memory: Organism, Myth, Text* (Berkeley: U of California P, 1992), 115–30.

8. Marcel Proust, *A la recherche du temps perdu,* 3 vols. (Paris: Gallimard, 1954); Proust, *Remembrance of Things* Past, 3 vols., trans. C. K. Scott-Moncrief and T. Kilmartin (New York: Vintage, 1982). Further references to the original and the translation are given in parentheses in the text.

9. Paul de Man, *Allegories of Reading* (New Haven: Yale UP, 1979), 78.

10. Gilles Deleuze and Felix Guattari, 'Le Rhyzome,' *Mille Plateaux* (Paris: Minuit, 1980), 17; Deleuze and Guattari, *A Thousand Plateaus,* trans. Brian Massumi (Minneapolis: U of Minnesota P, 1987), 10.

11. Charles Darwin, *The Various Contrivances by which Orchids Are Fertilized by Insects* 2d ed. (London: J. Murray, 1904), 285–86.

12. Charles Darwin, *The Effects of Cross- and Self-Fertilization in the Vegetable Kingdom* (New York: Appleton, 1877), 421.

13. Jean-Marie Pelt, *Les Plantes: Amours et civilisations végétales* (Paris: Marabout, 1980–81), 38.

14. Georges Poulet, 'Proust and Human Time,' in *Proust: A Collection of Critical Essays,* ed. René Girard (Englewood Cliffs, N.J.: Prentice Hall, 1962), 164.

15. All German citations of Rilke's poems come from *Sämtliche Werke,* 6 vols. (Wiesbaden: Insel Verlag, 1926), abbreviated sw. If not otherwise mentioned, the English translation comes from *The Selected Poetry of Rainer Maria Rilke,* trans. Stephen Mitchell (New York: Vintage, 1984). Page numbers for these two works are cited in the text.

16. Rilke, *Rilke/Lou Andreas-Salomé Briefwechsel,* ed. Ernst Pfeiffer (Frankfurt: Insel Verlag, 1975), 252–53; cited by Mitchell, in *Selected Poetry,* 312.

17. Letter 384, 'An Xaver Moss' (20 April 1923) in Rilke, *Briefe* (Wiesbaden: Insel Verlag, 1950), 833; cited in Mitchell, *Selected Poetry,* 336.

18. Johann Wolfgang von Goethe, *Botanical Writings,* trans. Bertha Müller (Honolulu: U of Hawaii P, 1952), 13, 24.

19. Elizabeth Sewell, *The Orphic Voice: Poetry and Natural History* (New Haven: Yale UP, 1960), 378.

20. Martin Heidegger, 'What Are Poets For?' in *Poetry, Language, Thought,* trans. Albert Hofstadter (New York: Harper and Row, 1975), 138, 132, 106.

21. Rilke, *Briefe,* 833; Mitchell, *Selected Poetry,* 336, my emphasis.

22. Heidegger, 'What Are Poets For?' 124.

23. Letter 17, 'An Franz Xaver Kappus' (April 23, 1903) in *Briefe,* 51; Rainer Maria Rilke, *Letters to a Young Poet,* trans. Stephen Mitchell (New York: Random House, 1984), 23–24.

24. Martin Heidegger, *Early Greek Thinking: The Dawn of Western Philosophy,* trans. David Farrell Krell and Frank A. Capuzzi (New York: Harper and Row, 1984), 114.

25. Rainer Maria Rilke, *Sonnets to Orpheus,* trans. Leslie Norris and Alan Keele (Columbia, Mo.: Camden House, 1984), 6. Hereafter the translations are cited in the text, by page number in *Sonnets.*

26. Herbert Marcuse, *Eros and Civilization: A Philosophical Enquiry into Freud* (New York: Vintage, 1955), 171.

27. Goethe, *Botanical Writings,* trans. Bertha Müller (Honolulu: U of Hawaii P, 1952), 129.

28. Heidegger, *Early Greek Thinking,* 63.

29. Ibid., 67.

30. Letter 24, 'An Franz Xaver Kappus' (May 14, 1904) in *Briefe,* 79; cited in Mitchell, *Selected Poetry,* 342.

31. Letter 31, 'An ein junges Mädchen' (November 20, 1904) in ibid., 104; cited in Mitchell, *Selected Poetry,* 337.

CHAPTER 3

1. Francis Ponge, *La Fabrique du pré* (Geneva: Editions d'art Albert Skira, 1971); Ponge, *The Making of the Pré,* trans. Lee Fahnenstock (Columbia, Mo.: U of Missouri P, 1979). Further references to this text and its translations are abbreviated FP and MP, respectively, with page/line numbers.

2. Clarence J. Hylander, *The World of Plant Life* (New York: Macmillan, 1939), 503–4.

3. Martin Heidegger, *An Introduction to Metaphysics,* trans. Ralph Manheim (New York: Anchor Books, 1961), 106, 96.

4. Philippe Sollers, *Entretiens avec Francis Ponge.* (Paris: Seuil, 1970), 41. Translations are mine.

5. Francis Ponge, *Le Parti pris des choses,* ed. Ian Higgins (London: Athlone Press, 1979), 68; Ponge, *The Voice of Things,* ed. and trans. Beth Archer (New York: McGraw-Hill, 1972), 63. All further references to this work and its

translation in the text use the abbreviations PPC and VT, with page numbers.

6. Jacques Derrida, *Signéponge/Signsponge,* trans. Richard Rand (New York: Columbia UP, 1984), 14–15.

7. Francis Ponge, *Le Grand Recueil,* II, 2 vols. (Paris: Gallimard, 1961), 250; my translation.

8. Sollers, *Entretiens,* 119. Robert W. Greene, 'Francis Ponge, Metapoet,' *Modern Language Notes* 85 (May 1970): 585.

9. Gilles Deleuze and Felix Guattari, *Mille Plateaux* (Paris: Minuit, 1980).

10. Renée Riese Hubert, 'Francis Ponge and Postmodern Illustration,' *Criticism* 30 (Summer 1988): 382. See my discussion in chapter 2.

11. Francis Ponge, *Pour un Malherbe* (Paris: Gallimard, 1965), 36. All further references in the text use the abbreviation PM; my translations.

12. Ponge, *Le Grand Recueil* II, 194, my translation.

13. Francis Ponge, *L'Atelier contemporain* (Paris: Gallimard, 1977), 221, my translation.

14. Ponge, *Le Grande Recueil,* I, 275, my translation.

15. Ponge, *Le Grand Recueil,* II, 224, my translation.

16. Cited in Jean Thibaudeau, *Francis Ponge* (Paris: Gallimard, 1967), 214, my translation.

17. Francis Ponge, *Proêmes* (Paris: Gallimard, 1948), 180, my translation.

18. Derrida, *Signéponge/Signsponge,* see 109–10.

19. Paul Valéry, 'Mélange,' *Oeuvres complètes,* 2 vols. (Paris: Gallimard, 1957–60), 2:384, my translation.

20. Deleuze and Guattari, *Mille Plateaux,* 51; Deleuze and Guattari, *A Thousand Plateaus,* trans. Brian Massumi (Minneapolis: U of Minnesota P, 1987), 37–38.

CHAPTER 4

1. Luce Irigaray, *Speculum de l'autre femme* (Paris: Minuit, 1974), 203; Irigaray, *Speculum of the Other Woman,* trans. Gillian C. Gill (Ithaca: Cornell UP, 1985), 162.

2. Luce Irigaray, *Ce Sexe qui n'en est pas un* (Paris: Minuit, 1977), 216 (abbreviated *Ce Sexe*). Irigaray, *This Sex Which Is*

Not One, trans. Catherine Porter and Carolyn Burke (Ithaca: Cornell UP, 1985), 217. Hereafter the page references to *Ce Sexe* and its translation are given in the text.

3. Jean-Jacques Rousseau, *Confessions* (Paris: Gallimard, 1959), 226; Rousseau, *The Confessions,* trans. J. M. Cohen (London: Penguin Books, 1953), 216.

4. Hélène Cixous, *Illa* (Paris: Des femmes, 1980), 157. Further references appear in parentheses in the text, along with my translations.

5. Jacques Derrida, 'Télépathie,' in *Psyché: Inventions de l'autre* (Paris: Galilée, 1987), 247; Derrida, 'Telepathy,' trans. Nicholas Royle, *Oxford Literary Review* 10 (1988): 146.

6. See Diane Griffin Crowder, 'Amazons and Mothers? Monique Wittig, Hélène Cixous and Theories of Women's Writing,' *Contemporary Literature* 24, 2 (1983): 143; Donna Stanton, 'Language and Revolution: The Franco-American Dis-Connection,' in *The Future of Difference,* ed. Hester Eisenstein and Alice Jardine (New Brunswick: Rutgers UP, 1985), 86; Ann Rosalind Jones, 'Writing the Body: Toward an Understanding of *L'Ecriture féminine,*' in *The New Feminist Criticism,* ed. Elaine Showalter (New York: Pantheon, 1985), 368–69. For a comprehensive study of Cixous's works, see Verena Andermatt Conley, *Hélène Cixous: Writing the Feminine* (Lincoln: University of Nebraska Press, 1984).

7. Ann Rosalind Jones, 'Inscribing Femininity: French Theories of the Feminine,' in *Making a Difference: Feminist Literary Criticism,* ed. Gayle Greene and Coppélia Kahn (London: Methuen, 1985), 92.

8. Hélène Cixous and Catherine Clément, *La Jeune née* (Paris: 10/18, 1975), 182, my translation.

9. Hélène Cixous, *Limonade tout était si infini* (Paris: Des femmes, 1982), 103 (abbreviated *Limonade* in the text references, along with my translations).

10. Ovid, *Metamorphoses,* trans. Rolfe Humphries (Bloomington: Indiana UP, 1967), 119.

11. 'The Homeric Hymns,' in *Hesiod, The Homeric Hymns, and*

Homerica, trans. Hugh G. Evelyn-White (Cambridge: Harvard UP, 1982), 289.

12. Ibid., 293.

13. Avital Ronell is inspired by Cixous when she writes, 'Maintaining and joining, the telephone line holds together what it separates. . . . The telephone was borne up by the invaginated structures of a mother's deaf ear. Still it was an ear that placed calls.' Ronell, *The Telephone Book: Technology–Schizophrenia–Electric Speech* (Lincoln: U of Nebraska P, 1991), 4–5.

14. Hélène Cixous, 'Castration or Decapitation,' trans. Annette Kuhn, *Signs* 7 (1981): 54.

15. Michel Leiris, 'Perséphone,' in *Biffures* (Paris: Gallimard, 1948), 85, my translation.

16. Ibid., 138.

17. Derrida, 'Télépathie,' 247–48; Derrida, 'Telepathy,' 8.

18. Jacques Derrida, *Ulysse gramophone* (Paris: Galilée, 1987). For a discussion of Derrida, Joyce, and flowers, see Sartilliot, 88–100.

19. Ibid., 84, my translations.

20. Ibid., 16, 109. Jacques Derrida, *Glas* (Paris: Galilée, 1974).

21. Hélène Cixous, *With ou l'art de l'innocence* (Paris: Des femmes, 1981), 268, my translation.

22. Hélène Cixous, 'De la scène de l'inconscient à la scène de l'Histoire: Chemin d'une écriture,' in *Hélène Cixous, chemins d'une écriture,* ed. Françoise Rossum-Guyon and Myriam Diaz-Diacretz (PUV St. Denis, 1990), 32, my translations.

23. Ibid., 16.

24. Hélène Cixous, *Portrait du soleil* (Paris: Denoël, 1973), 5, my translation.

Works Cited

Abraham, Nicolas, and Torok, Maria. *Cryptonymie: Le Verbier de l'homme aux loups.* Paris: Aubier Flammarion, 1976.

Bataille, Georges. 'Le Langage des fleurs.' *Oeuvres complètes.* 12 vols. Paris: Gallimard, 1970.

Bewell, Alan. 'Keats's "Realm of Flora."' *Studies in Romanticism* 31 (Spring 1992): 71–98.

Bonaparte, Marie. 'De la mort et des fleurs.' *Revue française de psychanalyse* 1 (1987): 321–35.

Cixous, Hélène. 'Castration or Decapitation.' Trans. Annette Kuhn. *Signs* 7 (1981): 41–55.

——. 'De la scène de l'inconscient à la scène de l'Histoire: Chemin d'une écriture.' In *Hélène Cixous, chemins d'une écriture,* ed. Françoise Rossum-Guyon and Miriam Diaz-Diacretz. Paris: PUV St Denis, 1990.

——. *Illa.* Paris: Des femmes, 1980.

——. *Limonade tout était si infini.* Paris: Des femmes, 1982.

——. *Portrait du soleil.* Paris: Denoël, 1973.

——. *With ou l'art de l'innocence.* Paris: Des femmes, 1981.

Cixous, Hélène, and Catherine Clément. *La Jeune née.* Paris: 10/18, 1975.

Conley, Verena Andermatt. *Hélène Cixous: Writing the Feminine.* Lincoln: University of Nebraska Press, 1984.

Crowder, Diane Griffin. 'Amazons and Mothers? Monique Wittig, Hélène Cixous and Theories of Women's Writing.' *Contemporary Literature* 24, 2 (1983): 117–44.

Darwin, Charles. *The Effects of Cross- and Self-Fertilization in the Vegetable Kingdom.* New York: Appleton, 1877.

——. *The Origin of Species.* New York: New American Library, 1958.

——. *The Various Contrivances by which Orchids Are Fertilized by Insects.* 2d ed. London: J. Murray, 1904.

Deleuze, Gilles, and Guatarri, Felix. 'Le Rhyzome.' *Mille Plateaux.* Paris: Minuit, 1980.

——. *A Thousand Plateaus.* Trans. Brian Massumi. Minneapolis: University of Minnesota Press, 1987.

Derrida, Jacques. *Glas.* Paris: Galilée, 1974.

——. *Glas.* Trans. John P. Leavey, Jr., and Richard Rand. Lincoln: Nebraska University Press, 1986.

——. 'La Mythologie blanche: La métaphore dans le texte philosophique.' *Marges de la philosophie.* Paris: Minuit, 1972.

——. *Margins of Philosophy.* Trans. Alan Bass. Chicago: Chicago University Press, 1982.

——. *Signéponge/Signsponge.* Trans. Richard Rand. New York: Columbia University Press, 1984.

——. 'Télépathie.' *Psyché: Inventions de l'autre.* Paris: Galilée, 1987.

——. 'Telepathy.' Trans. Nicholas Royle. *Oxford Literary Review* 10 (1988): 3–41.

——. *Ulysse gramophone.* Paris: Galilée, 1987.

Foucault, Michel. *Les Mots et les choses.* Paris: Gallimard, 1966.

——. *The Order of Things.* New York: Random House, 1973.

Freud, Sigmund. 'Die Traumdeutung.' *Gesammelte Werke,* vol.8. London: Imago, 1942.

——. *The Interpretation of Dreams.* Trans. James Strachey. New York: Avon, 1965.

Goethe, Johann Wolfgang von. *Botanical Writings.* Trans. Bertha Müller. Honolulu: University of Hawaii Press, 1952.

——. 'Die Metamorphose der Pflanzen.' *Werke,* vol.13. 5th ed. Hamburg: Christian Wegner Verlag, 1966.

Goody, Jack. 'The Secret Language of Flowers.' *Yale Journal of Criticism* 3 (1990): 133–52.

Gordon, Lesley. *Green Magic: Flowers, Plants, and Herbs in Lore and Legend.* New York: Vintage, 1977.

Greene, Robert W. 'Francis Ponge, Metapoet.' *Modern Language Notes* 85 (May 1970): 572–92.

Grieve, M. *A Modern Herbal.* New York: Hafner, 1971.

Hegel, G. W. F. 'Grundlinien der Philosophie des Rechts.' *Werke* 7. Frankfurt: Suhrkamp Verlag, 1970.

———. 'Phänomenologie des Geistes.' *Werke* 3. Frankfurt: Suhrkamp Verlag, 1970.

———. *The Phenomenology of Spirit.* Trans. A. V. Miller. Oxford: Oxford University Press, 1979.

———. *The Philosophy of Right.* Trans. T. M. Knox. Oxford: Oxford University Press, 1978.

Hesiod. *The Homeric Hymns, and Homerica.* Trans. Hugh G. Evelyn-White. Cambridge: Harvard University Press, 1982.

Heidegger, Martin. *Early Greek Thinking: The Dawn of Western Philosophy.* Trans. David Farrell Krell and Frank A. Capuzzi. New York: Harper and Row, 1984.

———. *An Introduction to Metaphysics.* Trans. Ralph Manheim. New York: Anchor Books, 1961.

———. 'What Are Poets For?' *Poetry, Language, Thought.* Trans. Albert Hofstadter. New York: Harper and Row, 1975.

Hubert, Renée Riese. 'Francis Ponge and Postmodern Illustration.' *Criticism* 30 (Summer 1988): 375–98.

Hylander, Clarence J. *The World of Plant Life.* New York: Macmillan, 1939.

Irigaray, Luce. *Ce Sexe qui n'en est pas un.* Paris: Minuit, 1977.

———. *Speculum de l'autre femme.* Paris: Minuit, 1974.

———. *Speculum of the Other Woman.* Trans. Gillian C. Gill. Ithaca: Cornell University Press, 1985.

———. *This Sex Which Is Not One.* Trans. Catherine Porter and Carolyn Burke. Ithaca: Cornell University Press, 1985.

Jones, Ann Rosalind. 'Writing the Body: Toward an Understanding of L'Ecriture féminine.' In *The New Feminist Criticism*, ed. Elaine Showalter. New York: Pantheon, 1985.

———. 'Inscribing Femininity: French Theories of the Feminine.' In *Making a Difference: Feminist Literary Criticism*, ed. Gayle Greene and Coppélia Kahn. London: Methuen, 1985.

Kuberski, Philip. 'Proust's Brain.' In his *Persistence of Memory: Organism, Myth, Text.* Berkeley: University of California Press, 1992.

Leiris, Michel. 'Perséphone.' *Biffures.* Paris: Gallimard, 1948.

Lévi-Strauss, Claude. *The Savage Mind.* Chicago: University of Chicago Press, 1968.

Man, Paul de. *Allegories of Reading.* New Haven: Yale University Press, 1979.

Macmillan, Hugh. *The Poetry of Plants.* London: Pitman, 1907.

Marcuse, Herbert. *Eros and Civilization: A Philosophical Enquiry into Freud.* New York: Vintage, 1955.

Ovid. *Metamorphoses.* Trans. Rolfe Humphries. Bloomington: Indiana University Press, 1967.

Pelt, Jean-Marie. *Les Plantes: Amours et civilisations végétales.* Paris: Marabout, 1980–81.

Ponge, Francis. *L'Atelier contemporain.* Paris: Gallimard, 1977.

———. *La Fabrique du pré.* Geneva: Editions d'art Albert Skira, 1971.

———. *Le Grand Receuil,* II (2 vols.). Paris: Gallimard, 1961.

———. *The Making of the Pré.* Trans. Lee Fahnenstock. Columbia: University of Missouri Press, 1979.

———. *Le Parti pris des choses.* Ed. Ian Higgins. London: Athlone Press, 1979.

———. *Pour un Malherbe.* Paris: Gallimard, 1965.

———. *Proêmes.* Paris: Gallimard, 1948.

———. *The Voice of Things.* Ed. and trans. Beth Archer. New York: McGraw-Hill, 1972.

Poulet, Georges. *L'Espace proustien.* Paris: Gallimard, 1963.

———. 'Proust and Human Time.' *Proust: A Collection of Critical Essays.* Ed. René Girard. Englewood Cliffs, N.J.: Prentice Hall, 1962.

Proust, Marcel. *A la recherche du temps perdu.* 3 vols. Paris: Gallimard, 1954.

———. *Remembrance of Things Past.* 3 vols. Trans. C. K. Scott-Moncrief and T. Kilmartin. New York: Vintage, 1982.

Rilke, Rainer Maria. *Briefe.* Wiesbaden: Insel Verlag, 1950.

———. *Letters to a Young Poet.* Trans. Stephen Mitchell. New York: Random House, 1984.

———. *Rilke/Lou Andreas-Salomé Briefwechsel.* Ed. Ernst Pfeiffer. Frankfurt: Insel Verlag, 1975.

———. *Sämtliche Werke.* 6 vols. Wiesbaden: Insel Verlag, 1926.

——. *The Selected Poetry of Rainer Marie Rilke.* Trans. Stephen Mitchell. New York: Vintage, 1984.

——. *Sonnets to Orpheus.* Trans. Leslie Norris and Alan Keele. Columbia, Mo.: Camden House, 1984.

Ronell, Avital. *The Telephone Book: Technology–Schizophrenia–Electric Speech.* Lincoln: University of Nebraska Press, 1991.

Rousseau, Jean-Jacques. *Le Botaniste sans maître ou: Manière d'apprendre seul la botanique.* Paris: Métaille, 1983.

——. *Confessions.* Paris: Gallimard 'Serie La Pleiade,' 1959.

——. *The Confessions.* Trans. J. M. Cohen. London: Penguin Books, 1953.

Ruskin, John. 'Proserpina.' *Complete Works,* vol.25. Ed. E. T. Cook and Alexander Wedderburn. London: Allen, 1906.

Sartiliot, Claudette. *Citation and Modernity: Derrida, Joyce, and Brecht.* Norman: University of Oklahoma Press, 1993.

Sewell, Elizabeth. *The Orphic Voice: Poetry and Natural History.* New Haven: Yale University Press, 1960.

Sollers, Philippe. *Entretiens avec Francis Ponge.* Paris: Seuil, 1970.

Stanton, Donna. 'Language and Revolution: The Franco-American Dis-Connection.' *The Future of a Difference.* Ed. Hester Eisenstein and Alice Jardine. New Brunswick: Rutgers University Press, 1985.

Thibaudeau, Jean. *Francis Ponge.* Paris: Gallimard, 1967.

Valéry, Paul. 'Mélange.' *Oeuvres complètes.* 2 vols. Paris: Gallimard, Series 'La Pleiade,' 1957–60.

Index

Other volumes in the series Texts and Contexts include: